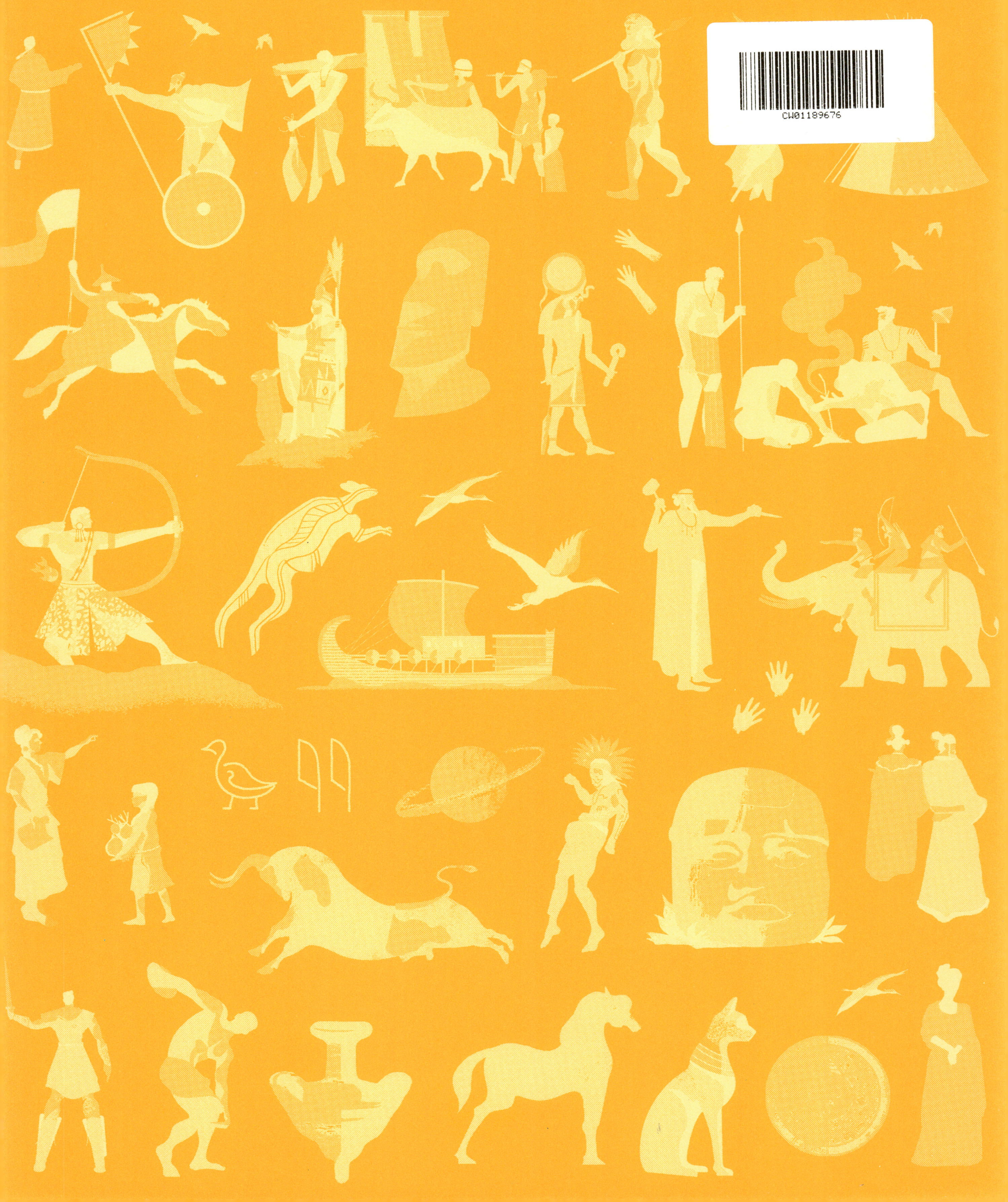

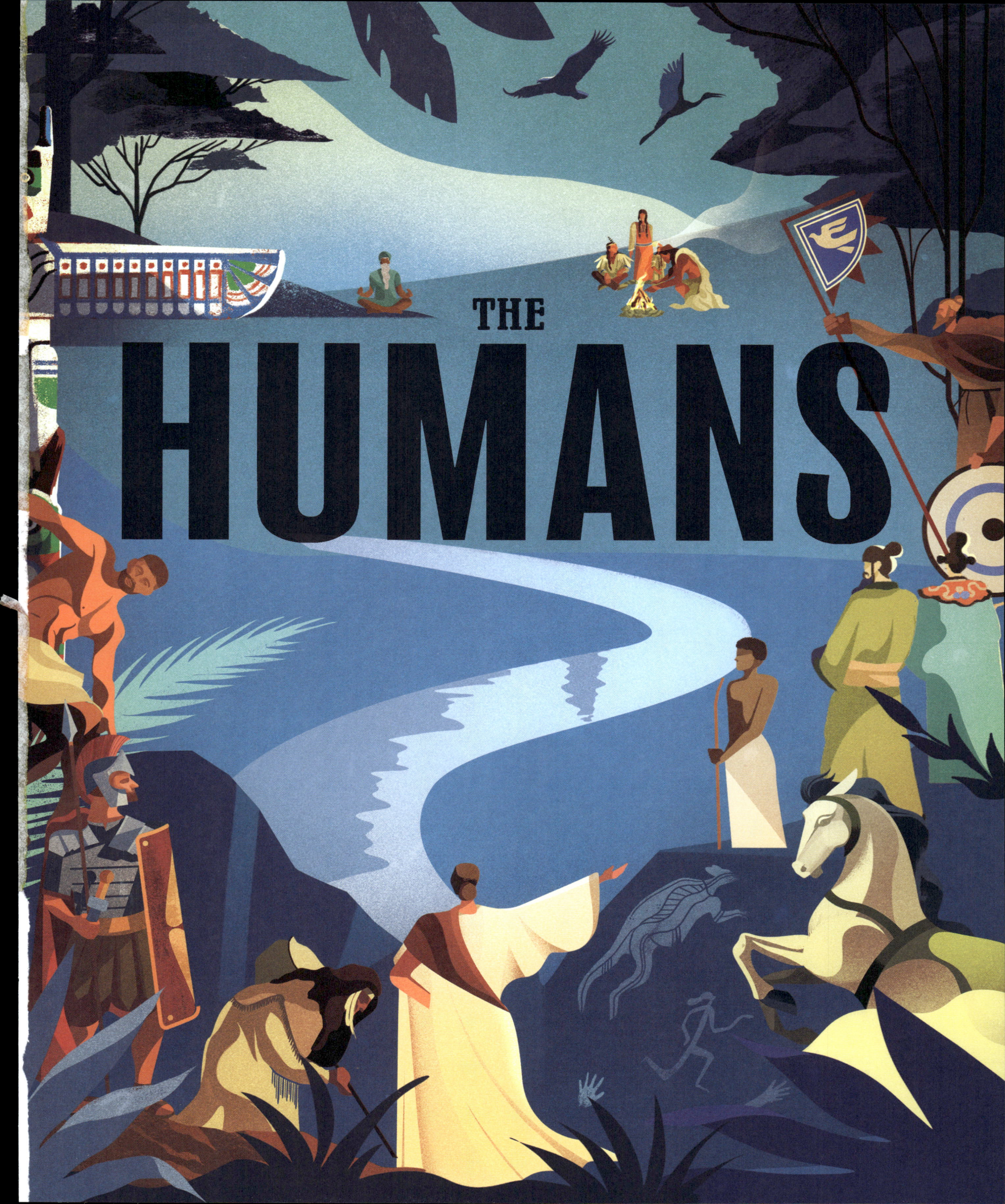

THE HUMANS

WRITTEN BY
JONNY MARX

ILLUSTRATED BY
CHARLIE DAVIS

The world is an ever-changing place and the people within it are capable of incredible things; discoveries are made, records are broken, new facts are found and history recovered. We will be happy to revise and update information in future editions.

The Forest Stewardship Council® (FSC®) is an international, non-governmental organisation dedicated to promoting responsible management of the world's forests. FSC operates a system of forest certification and product labelling that allows consumers to identify wood and wood-based products from well-managed forests and other controlled sources.

For more information about the FSC, please visit their website at www.fsc.org

FSC
www.fsc.org
MIX
From responsible sources
FSC® C124807

360 DEGREES
An imprint of the Little Tiger Group
1 Coda Studios, 189 Munster Road, London SW6 6AW
www.littletiger.co.uk
First published in Great Britain 2020
Text by Jonny Marx
Text copyright © Caterpillar Books Ltd 2020
Illustrations copyright © Charlie Davis 2020
A CIP catalogue record for this book is available from the British Library
All rights reserved
Printed in China
ISBN: 978-1-84857-993-4
CPB/2700/1368/0120
10 9 8 7 6 5 4 3 2 1

LITTLE TIGER
LONDON

INTRODUCTION

The human species, as we know it today, has existed for approximately 200,000 years. Though we still look similar to our ancient ancestors, we now behave very differently!

In the last 50,000 years, our species has created thousands of written and verbal languages; we've followed religions; built structures, settlements, villages, cities and civilisations; we've created stories to be passed from generation to generation; climbed mountains, crossed deserts and journeyed far and wide; we've invented transport, technology and cures for diseases; we've written songs, created instruments, art and music; we've even cultivated cultures that still exist today.

This book takes a glimpse at the origin of our species: where we came from, how we used to behave and why we've now traversed the globe, and an in-depth gaze into the great inventions our ancestors created for the benefit of the human race. We'll look at the rise and fall of some of the ancient civilisations and the lessons they've taught us.

From the Nubians to the Native Americans, and the Akkadians to the ancient Egyptians, our predecessors have given us all sorts of incredible inventions, technologies and practices.

Let's delve into the past and discover exactly what the humans have done for us …

CONTENTS

Where It All Began	4
The Genus	6
Map of Species Movement	7
Stone, Bronze and Iron Ages	8
Africa	**9**
The Nubians	10
The Egyptians	12
The Phoenicians	16
What About the Rest of Africa?	18
Oceania	**19**
The Aboriginal Australians	20
The Micronesians and Melanesians	22
The Polynesians	24
Western Asia	**25**
The Sumerians	26
The Akkadians	29
The Assyrians	30
The Babylonians	31
The Persians	32
Eastern Asia	**33**
The People of the Indus Valley	34
The Ancient Chinese	36
The Mongols	39
What About the Rest of Asia?	40
Europe	**41**
The Minoans	42
The Ancient Greeks	43
The Romans	46
The Celts	49
The Vikings	50
The Americas	**52**
The Native Americans	53
The Olmecs	56
The Maya	57
The Inca	59
The Aztecs	60
Timeline	62
What Came Next?	64

WHERE IT ALL BEGAN

Many other species similar to our kind lived in the world before us. Let's dig through history and see where human life began.

Some of the Latin names that we attribute to animals and plants can be quite confusing, so before we look at the characteristics that make humankind so unique, let's familiarise ourselves with some useful information:

SPECIES VS GENUS

This is *Tyrannosaurus rex*. It belongs to the *Tyrannosaurus* **genus** and is the *rex* **species**. Many other dinosaurs exist in the *Tyrannosaurus* **genus**.

This is *Homo sapiens* (human beings, just like us). We belong to the *Homo* **genus**, and we are the *sapiens* **species**. Other types of hominin exist in the *Homo* genus ...

EVOLUTION

Species evolve over time, adapting and changing over the course of thousands of years. Evolution can make animals stronger, cleverer, smaller, taller, fatter, thinner, or change their behaviour altogether.

A **primate** is a classification of mammal, which includes humans, apes and monkeys.

Several million years ago, humans evolved from apes. Some primates changed the way they moved by walking on two legs. Known as bipedalism, this adjustment occurred approximately four to six million years ago and is one of the key characteristics of humankind today.

AUSTRALOPITHECUS

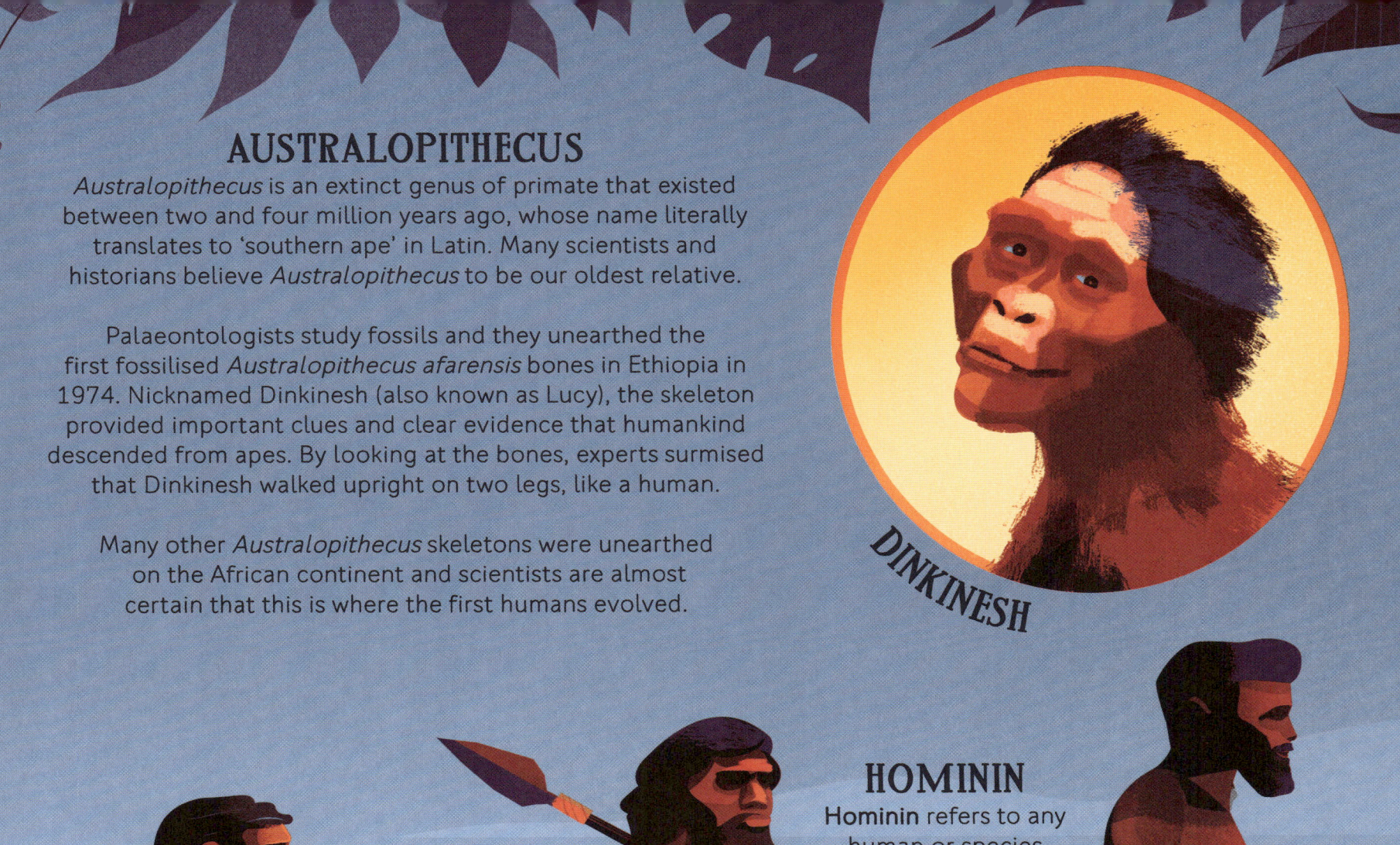

Australopithecus is an extinct genus of primate that existed between two and four million years ago, whose name literally translates to 'southern ape' in Latin. Many scientists and historians believe *Australopithecus* to be our oldest relative.

Palaeontologists study fossils and they unearthed the first fossilised *Australopithecus afarensis* bones in Ethiopia in 1974. Nicknamed Dinkinesh (also known as Lucy), the skeleton provided important clues and clear evidence that humankind descended from apes. By looking at the bones, experts surmised that Dinkinesh walked upright on two legs, like a human.

Many other *Australopithecus* skeletons were unearthed on the African continent and scientists are almost certain that this is where the first humans evolved.

DINKINESH

HOMININ
Hominin refers to any human or species closely related to humans.

DIVERSITY
As time passed, our species changed. Humans bred with other hominins, creating a diverse group of people.

The only species of human alive today is *Homo sapiens*.

THE GENUS

Early human species are still being discovered and our understanding of their relationship with one another is constantly changing. What we're almost certain of, however, is that the first species of the *Homo* genus evolved 2.5 million years ago in Africa. Over the course of a couple of million years, other human species evolved, moving gradually across the globe. These modern humans were the most intelligent beings on the planet, but *Homo sapiens* swiftly became the most dominant.

DID YOU KNOW?
Our ancient ancestors were not always competitors. In 2018, an ancient bone belonging to a teenage girl was discovered in a Siberian cave. When scientists analysed the bone, they realised the girl had a Neanderthal mother and a Denisovan father.

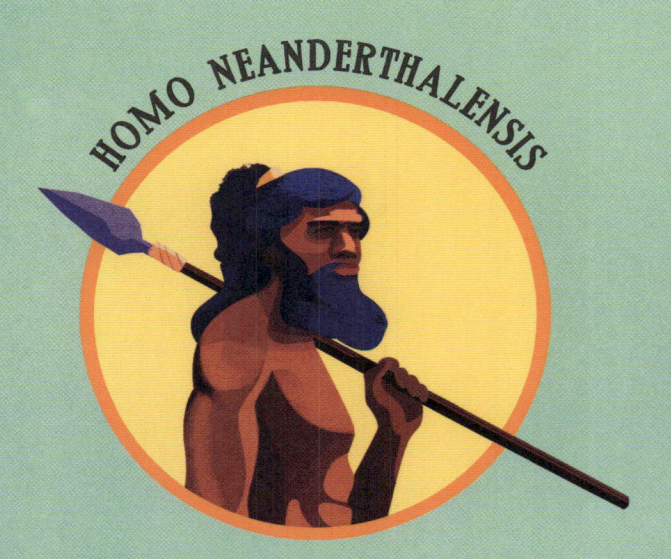

HOMO NEANDERTHALENSIS

Neanderthals evolved approximately 400,000 years ago in Eurasia. They were muscular, powerful, and their brains were actually larger than our brains today.

Their remains were first discovered in the Neander Valley in Germany. The species died out roughly 40,000 years ago.

HOMO FLORESIENSIS

Homo floresiensis fossils are native to the island of Flores in Indonesia. This species stood at about 1m (3ft) in stature, weighing little more than 20-30kg (45-66lb).

Well-suited to scarce resources and island life, *Homo floresiensis* existed until just 50,000 years ago.

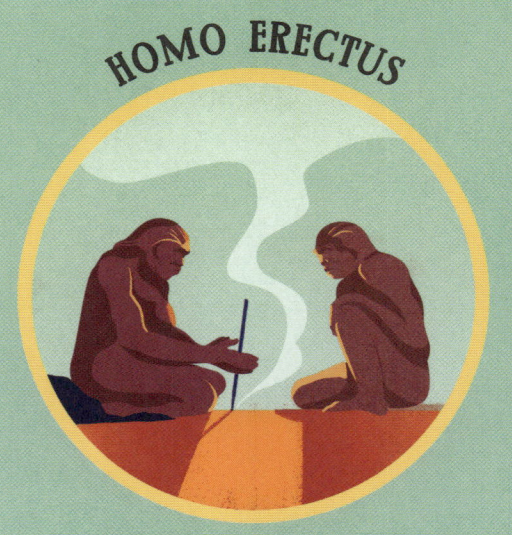

HOMO ERECTUS

Homo erectus means 'upright man' in Latin. This species existed for approximately 1.5 million years, making it the longest-lived of all the human species.

Homo erectus was possibly the first human species to wield and domesticate fire.

HOMO HEIDELBERGENSIS

HOMO RUDOLFENSIS

HOMO HABILIS

HOMO NALEDI

Many other species exist in the *Homo* genus and more are being discovered. There is fierce debate amongst scientists and historians as to whether some of these species should, in fact, be classified separately. Many have been identified from tiny bone fragments and it is not always clear whether a bone is from a new species.

HOMO SAPIENS
We are Homo sapiens ('wise man' in Latin).

Today, just one species of human exists ... us! Our existence sparked the demise of many other animals (including other human species!). Experts aren't certain as to why the rest of the species in the *Homo* genus became extinct, but it's plausible that the dominance of *sapiens* led to their downfall, combined with changes in climate and the emergence of diseases.

Our ability to adapt to changing climates and conditions may have also played an important part in our survival. The *sapiens* species was smaller and less muscular than the likes of *Homo neanderthalensis*, meaning fewer calories were required to survive. Or perhaps other species were just in the wrong place at the wrong time. The Neanderthals, for instance, were caught in a European permafrost during the Ice Age and may have perished as a result.

MAP OF SPECIES MOVEMENT
Homo sapiens rapidly became the most dominant human species and spread to all corners of the globe.

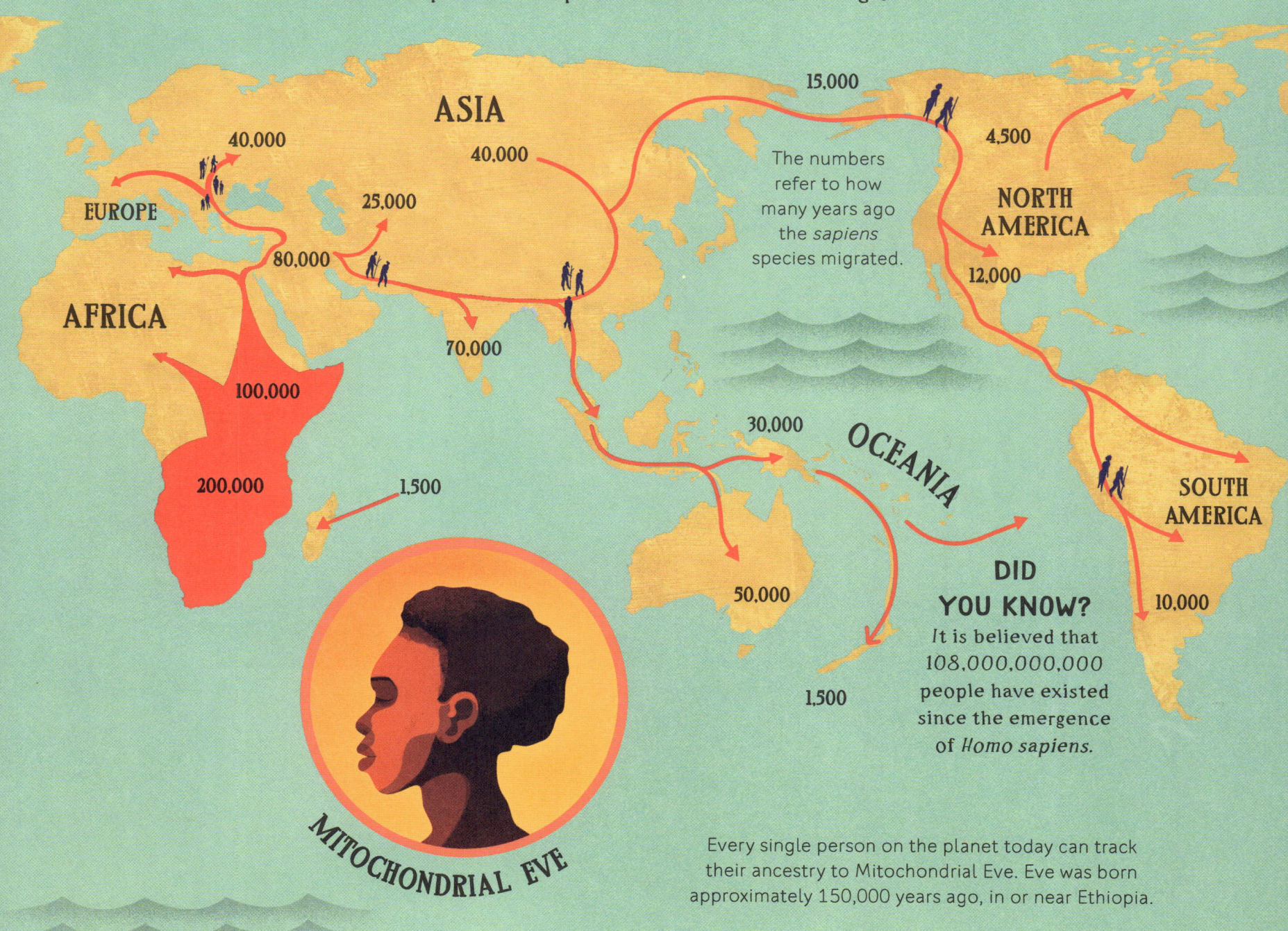

EUROPE 40,000
ASIA 40,000
25,000
15,000
NORTH AMERICA 4,500
12,000
AFRICA 80,000
100,000
200,000
70,000
1,500
30,000
OCEANIA
50,000
1,500
SOUTH AMERICA 10,000

The numbers refer to how many years ago the *sapiens* species migrated.

MITOCHONDRIAL EVE

DID YOU KNOW?
It is believed that 108,000,000,000 people have existed since the emergence of *Homo sapiens*.

Every single person on the planet today can track their ancestry to Mitochondrial Eve. Eve was born approximately 150,000 years ago, in or near Ethiopia.

STONE AGE
Circa 3.3 million years BCE – 3000 BCE

During the Stone Age, early human species used primitive stone tools to help them. *It was also during this time that the first farms were cultivated as humankind moved away from the hunter-gatherer lifestyle.*

BRONZE AGE
Circa 4000 BCE – 1200 BCE

Settlements in what we now call Turkey began to meld metals in approximately 4000 BCE, creating a tough material called bronze that transformed the creation of tools, weapons, armour and art for humankind.

IRON AGE
Circa 1200 BCE – 50 CE

Metalwork using iron became commonplace in 1200 BCE, and by the turn of the millenium iron was used readily throughout Europe. This durable metal led to better farming techniques and more advanced technnology.

WHAT HAPPENED NEXT?

Though *Homo sapiens* had now cornered the globe, it wasn't until the Bronze Age that it could create a record of its own history. Written languages, art, architecture and inventions would eventually follow, and civilisations would spring up simultaneously across the globe.

Many cultures are buried and archaeologists are still discovering the remains of ancient cities, towns and settlements. Based on our current discoveries, some of the oldest art can be found in Africa and Australia, the remnants of the oldest civilisations are in Africa and the Middle East and the most sophisticated feats of engineering were established in Asia.

Let's take a closer look at some of the most iconic peoples and civilisations to grace the planet …

Africa

Homo sapiens evolved on the African continent approximately 200,000 years ago. Small bands of people travelled across the African plains, forming roaming tribes that gradually moved northwards. It is thought that our species stayed within the confines of these lands for more than 100,000 years before migrating north into the Middle East and then beyond.

Roughly 8,000 years ago, the foundations for the world's first sophisticated civilisations bloomed along the banks of the River Nile. With access to fresh water, farming and trade eventually flourished and many incredible feats of engineering and architecture took place between 5000 and 3000 BCE.

THE NUBIANS

African people from what is now the Sahara region began to move towards the River Nile in Nubia (modern day Sudan) in approximately 5000 BCE.

One of the first cradles of civilisation, Nubia was brimming with gold, incense, ebony, ivory and other precious commodities. The Nubians used these to trade with other tribes and peoples, including the Egyptians in around 3000 BCE.

WHERE IN THE WORLD?

The first settlers to move towards the River Nile adapted from hunter-gatherers to fishermen and farmers. This gave them a more reliable food resource and this stability allowed the people to thrive along the river's edge.

NUBIA AND EGYPT

The Nubian and Egyptian people lived in relative harmony for many years, trading goods and sharing resources, but life was tough in this region.

Nubians and Egyptians began to jostle for trade routes and territory, prompting invasions and wars between the two. Between 2800 and 2300 BCE, for instance, the Nubians may have been forced out of Lower Nubia by the Egyptians.

AFRICA

MEDITERRANEAN SEA

EGYPT

LOWER NUBIA

RIVER NILE

UPPER NUBIA

RED SEA

MIDDLE EAST

Nubia was divided into two regions.

Because the Nile flows northwards, the southern part of the territory was known as **Upper Nubia** (or Kush) and the northern part was known as **Lower Nubia** (or Wawat).

Not only did the river allow people to access water and fertile land, it also provided the means to transport heavy goods over long distances, improving trade with surrounding areas.

Over time, African people from all across the south flocked towards the regions straddling the Nile. Nubia's population was, therefore, incredibly diverse.

MEROITIC ALPHABET
Nubians helped develop the Meroitic alphabet. As the language is so old, however, few people alive today can understand their ancient writings.

NUBIAN PYRAMIDS
There are almost twice as many pyramids in Sudan as in Egypt, and the debate as to who built theirs first is hotly contested amongst historians. Pyramid-like structures were built by many separate cultures and civilisations around the world, including the Aztecs, the Assyrians and the Romans!

Nubian armies were famed for their archery skills.

THE A-GROUP
The A-Group was the earliest known Nubian culture, existing from approximately 3800-2800 BCE. We know little about their way of life, but archaeologists discovered a host of A-Group burial sites, containing some exquisitely intricate pots, figurines, artefacts and carvings, along the banks of the Nile in the 1960s.

It is thought that the A-Group formed some of the first trade routes and even managed to acquire olive oil from the Mediterranean.

QUSTUL
Archaeologists found several tombs in a place called Qustul. Some of the graves belonged to Nubian rulers and officials.

Although most of these tombs had been looted and few objects remained, archaeologists did find an incense burner, ornately carved with pictures of boats, creatures and deities. It is a staggering 5,000 years old!

THE EGYPTIANS

The ancient Egyptians made vast architectural, agricultural, religious and technological advances during their time. They built towering pyramids, cultivated the land along the banks of the River Nile, fostered an elaborate religious system and even created a material similar to paper called papyrus.

The civilisation thrived from 3100 BCE until it was eventually absorbed into the Roman Empire in 30 BCE.

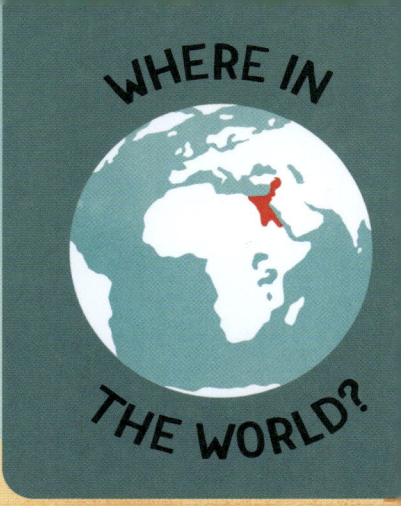

WHERE IN THE WORLD?

HIEROGLYPHICS

The Egyptians created a pictorial written language focussing on sounds, rather than letters. Ironically, the word 'hieroglyphics' is actually Greek, not Egyptian, and means 'holy marks'.

Linguists had trouble translating hieroglyphs until the discovery of the Rosetta Stone in 1799. The stone was inscribed with three scripts (one of which was ancient Greek), and each passage of text said roughly the same thing. Experts used their understanding of the Greek alphabet to translate the hieroglyphs, and the rest is history!

The Egyptians created hundreds of hieroglyphs.

MEDICAL INSTRUMENTS

The ancient Egyptians are credited with the creation of many medical tools, including a hook used to pluck chunks of brain out through a corpse's nose during mummification! They stored organs in special vessels known as canopic jars.

QEBHSENUEF
The falcon-headed god protected the intestines.

DUAMUTEF
The jackal-headed god looked after the stomach.

IMSETY
The human-headed god protected the liver.

HAPY
This baboon-headed god was in charge of the lungs.

IMHOTEP

Imhotep was an architect, physician, astrologer, adviser and all-round genius! He served a pharaoh called Djoser and is credited as being the brains behind the building of a structure called the Step Pyramid in approximately 2600 BCE. The pyramid was a staggering 60m (200ft) high and can still be seen today. It even housed an elaborate labyrinth.

HATSHEPSUT

Hatshepsut was one of Egypt's first female pharaohs. During her initial years as leader, statues were created, portraying her as a woman. Later on, however, depictions showed her as a muscular man with a false beard. How could this be?

Imhotep's architectural prowess was lauded by the ancient Egyptians, and many years after his death he was regarded as a demigod and later as a god in his own right!

Unfortunately, after Hatshepsut's death, her stepson destroyed as many statues of her as he could and removed her name from carvings and records. As a result, her history remained buried for a few thousand years! It wasn't until the 19th century (CE) that archaeologists and linguists began to unravel the mystery.

EMBALMING

The ancient Egyptians believed that life continued long after death, so they sometimes preserved dead bodies in a process called embalming or mummification, which could take up to 70 days to complete.

First, a corpse's guts and organs were placed in jars and the body was then soaked in salt solution before being wrapped in bandages. The Egyptians' attention to detail and care when preserving their dead is unrivalled.

SARCOPHAGUS

Egyptian pharaohs were buried in ornate coffins known as sarcophagi. The most famous sarcophagus belonged to Tutankhamun. His inner casket was adorned with more than 110kg (240lb) of gold and is the most expensive coffin ever discovered – it would be worth millions of pounds in today's money.

PAPYRUS
The Egyptians created a paper-like material from the papyrus plant, which grew in the fertile soil by the River Nile. The precise technique used is unknown, but it is thought that plants were harvested, dried and the stems split to create strips of material that could be layered and compressed. The Egyptians used papyrus to create scrolls.

TOOTHPASTE
An ancient recipe for toothpaste was discovered on a scrap of papyrus in the dark basement of a museum in Vienna, Austria, in 2003. The recipe dated from the 4th century CE, when the Romans ruled Egypt. Toothpaste may have existed before this, but the Egyptian recipe was advanced for its time:

One part rock salt
Two parts mint
One part dried iris flower
A dash of pepper

FURNITURE
Furniture in ancient times was a luxury, but the Egyptians are credited with inventing many of the items we may take for granted today, including chairs, tables, beds and chests, not to mention the coffins that some of their royals were buried in.

Trees were an extremely precious commodity in ancient Egypt and wood was scarce. It is thought that the Egyptians procured their wood from more fertile lands, especially Lebanon where cedar trees grew in abundance.

PETS
The Egyptians were fond of domesticating animals, especially cats, which helped get rid of household pests!

They regarded their pets with such esteem that some were mummified or buried with their owners. The Egyptians even created a pet cemetery in the city of Abydos.

DID YOU KNOW?
The Great Pyramid of Khufu took approximately 20 years to build.

DID YOU KNOW?
The temple of a god called Sobek was famously full of crocodiles.

Dogs were also popular pets, particularly with hunters and police, but there's evidence to suggest that all sorts of animals were kept in ancient Egypt, including baboons, fish, birds, lions and hippos!

POLICE

A stone carving dating back almost 4,500 years was discovered in the Saqqara burial ground in Egypt. The image depicts a scene of a policeman detaining a criminal with the help of his trusted companion, a baboon.

Police were originally used by pharaohs for personal security, but later to maintain public order. The Egyptians even hired bands of Nubian Medjay warriors armed with wooden clubs to form an elite police force.

GODS AND GODDESSES

The Egyptians worshipped several deities ... hundreds in fact! Many of their gods and goddesses were depicted with animal heads that embodied their characteristics.

RA

Ra was often shown with the head of a falcon, crowned by the Sun.

Ra was the god of the Sun. He was believed to have created the world and the Egyptians thought he died each night, only to be reborn at sunrise.

ANUBIS

The god of the dead had the head of a jackal. Anubis was credited with the invention of the embalming process.

THOTH

Thoth was the god of learning, writing and the inventor of languages. He was often depicted with the head of a bird called an ibis.

THE PHOENICIANS

The first Phoenician settlers were from the Middle East but the empire expanded into Africa and Europe, using the Mediterranean Sea as a bazaar in which to travel and trade. The Phoenician ports would have been stocked with spices, precious metals, foods, fabrics, timber, livestock, arts and crafts. Their ships spanned three continents to acquire and scatter goods.

MUREX SHELL

TRADE

The Phoenicians accumulated a great wealth by trading along a vast network of shipping routes. Their settlements were strategically built in parts of north Africa, the Middle East and southern Europe. All sorts of things were traded, including glassware, wood and furniture, but also more unusual items, including a purple dye made from murex shells that the Grecian upper classes used to colour their togas and tunics.

EUROPE

CARTHAGE

Carthage was built in the 9th century BCE and was one of the largest cities of its time. It was the epicentre of trade for the Phoenicians and its geographical placement was perfect. A large population could be sustained thanks to the proximity of a huge freshwater lake and the sea.

Carthage was eventually invaded and Phoenician buildings destroyed by the Romans during the Punic Wars. The Romans then rebuilt the metropolis in their own style and some of their ruins can be found in modern-day Tunis, Tunisia.

AFRICA

ALPHABET

Though the Sumerians were the first to create a written language, the Phoenicians were the first to develop an alphabet, where letters (consonants and vowels) could be ordered to create different sounds. Incorporating 22 letters, their alphabet would eventually influence the Greek alphabet and the alphabet we use today.

WHERE IN THE WORLD?

PHOENICIAN VASE

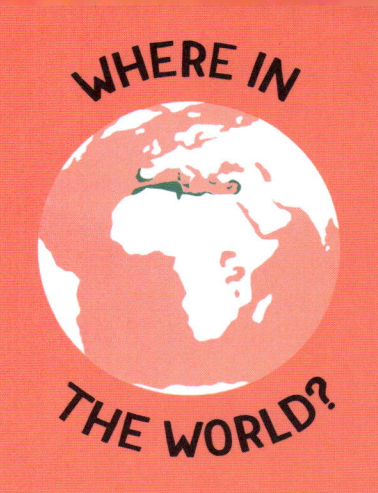

GLASSWARE

The first glass used by humans was obsidian, also known as volcanic glass. Obsidian is formed when hot magma and gases heat sand beneath the Earth's surface. This product is then spat out when the volcano erupts, and cools to form a solid mass. Obsidian was used to make arrowheads, jewellery and art more than 6,000 years ago.

It wasn't until 3500 BCE, however, in Egypt and Mesopotamia, that humans discovered how to produce their own glass in ovens and kilns. The Phoenicians then used bellows to create furnaces that could reach scorching temperatures. They also experimented with glass production, eventually 'blowing' the material to create hollow vessels, such as jugs, vases and perfume bottles.

MIDDLE EAST

MEDITERRANEAN SEA

DID YOU KNOW?

The Phoenicians were the best ship builders of their time. They needed hundreds of ships to support their trade network.

WHAT ABOUT THE REST OF AFRICA?

As Africa is where humankind initially evolved, why aren't remnants of civilisations dotted around everywhere? Historians have uncovered a wealth of cultures across the continent, but there may be many ancient settlements waiting to be discovered ...

MALI EMPIRE

The Mali Empire was centred around two great cities, Djenné and Timbuktu. The latter housed a huge library with more than half a million books.

Today, the largest mud building in the world can be found in Djenné.

SONGHAI EMPIRE

At its largest, the Songhai Empire was bigger than Western Europe, covering an area several hundred miles across.

Mansa Mūsā, the empire's ruler, is rumoured to have said that the kingdom would take a whole year to traverse.

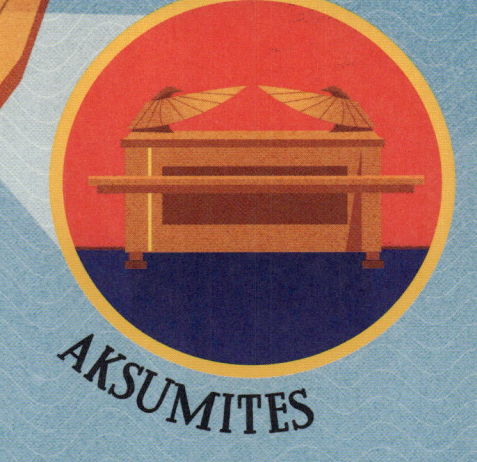

BANTU PEOPLE

The Bantu migrated out of what we now call Nigeria, moving through territories surrounding the Sahara, travelling as far as South Africa and Mozambique.

AKSUMITES

The Kingdom of Aksum was one of the world's great superpowers from 1st century CE to 7th century CE.

The Ark of the Covenant, a gold-covered chest said to contain the stone tablets inscribed with the Ten Commandments intrinsic to the Christian and Jewish religions, is reputedly buried in Aksum, the capital city.

DID YOU KNOW?

In 2018, archaeologists found what they believe to be the world's oldest drawing in Blombos Cave in South Africa. The artwork was scribbled on a rock using a pigment called ochre, and is believed to be more than 70,000 years old.

The presence of water is vital for a civilisation to flourish. Though the Sahara used to be verdant, the climate changed roughly 6,000 years ago. As fertile areas of Africa became hot and arid, it would have been difficult for humans to migrate towards large bodies of water or rivers, or to forsake the haven of the River Nile in order to search for other lands. Most archaeological finds have been close to the Nile, but plenty of other African societies and civilisations existed!

Oceania

Evidence suggests that a group of people, known as Melanesians, travelled from Southern Asia into Oceania roughly 50,000 years ago, navigating a network of pathways that have long since been submerged by rising sea levels. This extraordinary expedition allowed these intrepid explorers to inhabit and spread across the vast island of Australia, as well as some other neighbouring islands, including New Guinea.

Once sea levels rose, in approximately 6000 BCE, populations were locked in relative isolation until 4000 BCE, when tribes began to span the seas. It was at this time that a second wave of humans from Asia traversed straits of the Pacific Ocean, populating other islands surrounding Indonesia and the Philippines.

THE ABORIGINAL AUSTRALIANS

The Aboriginals were the first humans to inhabit Australia. They travelled across the enormous land mass, creating small settlements and societies along the way, each with its own dialect and identity. The Australian Aboriginals established the world's first culture with its own unique belief system, iconic art style and music. The island's location allowed the Aboriginals to live in isolation, away from human invaders, helping to preserve their distinct way of life.

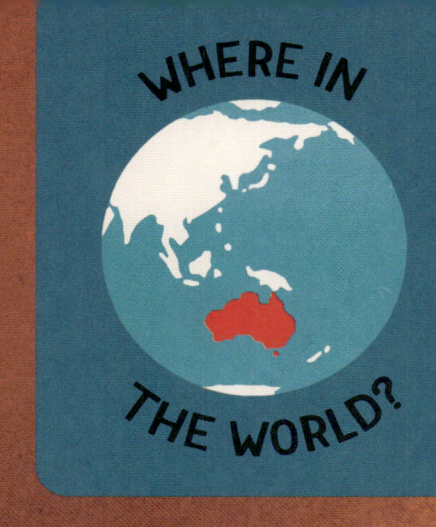

WHERE IN THE WORLD?

When European explorers settled on Australian shores, more than 250 different Aboriginal dialects existed.

DID YOU KNOW?
Painted depictions of the Rainbow Serpent have been found in Australian caves. Some of the pictures are thought to be 8,000 years old.

DID YOU KNOW?
'Aboriginal' means 'indigenous' or 'original inhabitant' in Latin.

TOOLS
The world's oldest axe was found during an archaeological dig in 2017 in Kakadu, in the Northern Territory of Australia. The axe was probably fashioned approximately 65,000 years ago, more than 15,000 years before other cultures learned how to craft similar tools themselves. The Australian Aboriginals also created spear heads made from bone or rock, boomerangs and tools to sharpen their weapons.

THE DREAMING

The Australian Aboriginal people wove an elaborate belief system known as The Dreaming, focussing on the creation of the world and the birth of humankind and mythical entities, including the Rainbow Serpent.

The Rainbow Serpent is said to have created the planet's rivers and mountains. It used its colossal body to push earth and rock and to gouge channels in which water could flow. According to Aboriginal lore, the enormous snake could also trigger storms and floods and its invigorating powers helped create humankind.

STORYTELLING

Before the creation of paper, or even a fully-formed written language, the only means of telling stories was through speech. Many Aboriginal tales were passed from generation to generation for thousands of years.

According to experts, Aboriginal Australians even discussed the news, commenting on changes in climate and rising sea levels more than 7,000 years ago. Geologists have discovered evidence that the sea surrounding Australia may have indeed risen by up to 120m (394ft) between 14,000 and 5000 BCE.

RAINBOW SERPENT

Many Aboriginal people today pay homage to The Dreaming and to their ancient ancestors through songs, stories, dances and ceremonies.

ART

Aboriginal cave paintings are some of the oldest in the world (many were created 40,000 years ago).

The Aboriginals used pigments called ochres combined with clay to paint their pictures and created different hues and shades by mixing ochres with other minerals.

Many artists today draw their inspiration from Aboriginal art and the iconic imagery created in caves is said to have inspired the likes of Claude Monet, Pablo Picasso and Paul Klee.

MUSICAL INSTRUMENTS

The didgeridoo is perhaps the world's oldest musical instrument. Invented by Aboriginal Australians, the wooden tubes were originally created from tree trunks or branches hollowed by termites and other burrowing insects. The didgeridoo's unique sound is created when air is blown through one end.

THE MICRONESIANS AND MELANESIANS

Though some of the thousands of islands that comprise Micronesia and Melanesia were inhabited roughly 40,000 years ago, the majority of the land masses weren't explored until 3,000-4,000 years ago as trailblazers from Indonesia, China and Australia took to the seas in search of new land. By approximately 700 CE, explorers had spread across almost all of the previously uninhabited islands.

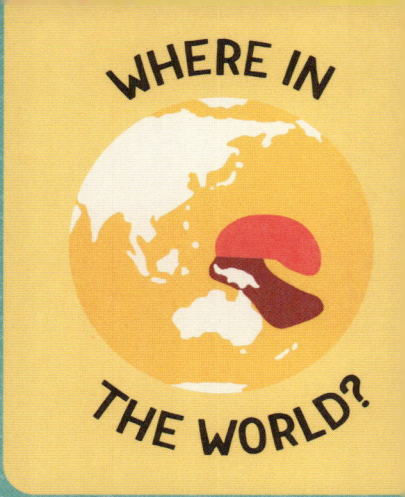

WHERE IN THE WORLD?

THE ISLANDS

Thousands of islands and archipelagos are scattered across this vast area of Pacific Ocean, including New Guinea, Fiji, Kiribati, Vanuatu and Nauru. When settlers sailed to these lands, many established their own independent cultures on separate islands. Each was left to grow and evolve for hundreds of years. As a result, almost all of the islands in this region of the world speak their own individual languages and dialects (yet none of these have alphabets).

When European settlers voyaged to Micronesia and Melanesia in the 1600s, languages became yet more varied.

DID YOU KNOW?

On the Melanesian island of West Papua, more than 250 ethnic groups reside, speaking more than 270 languages collectively.

Some historians believe West Papua was first inhabited 40,000 years ago – much earlier than many other islands in this region.

RIDING THE WAVES

In order to travel between treacherous sandbanks, reefs and over rip-roaring waves, the islanders built unique sailing vessels. Their outrigger canoes had special support beams and flotation devices to boost stability in swaying seas.

DID YOU KNOW?

An archaeological site known as Nan Madol can be found on the Micronesian island of Pohnpei. It is the only discovered ancient settlement to have been built atop a coral reef.

MICRONESIA

NAN MADOL

MELANESIA

The island cultures here remained intact until foreign settlers landed on the shores in the late 17th and 18th centuries, transforming many of the practices, languages and religions. European conquistadors (explorers) and travellers also introduced foreign diseases, disrupting the population on many of the islands. The number of native Chamorro people, for instance, fell from 100,000 to just a few thousand after a war with Spanish invaders during the late 1600s.

Despite foreign invasion and influences, islanders still retain many of the same cultural values as their ancestors.

DID YOU KNOW?

Of the three main cultural groups of this area of the Pacific Ocean, Melanesia is believed to be the first in which humans settled.

THE POLYNESIANS

Humankind began its journey to populate the Polynesian islands around 3,500 years ago as seafaring explorers travelled from the likes of Indonesia, Taiwan and the Philippines to land masses including Easter Island, Samoa, Niue and many more. There are thousands of Polynesian islands in total, but some of them have only recently been populated.

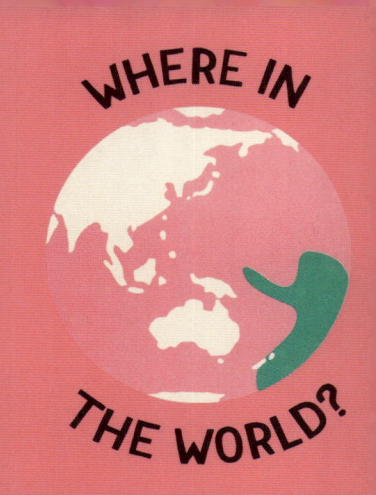

WHERE IN THE WORLD?

DID YOU KNOW?
Many animals and plants became extinct as a result of human settlement. This happened on a global scale and on every isle inhabited by *Homo sapiens*. On the remote Polynesian island of Rapa Nui, for example, bird and tree species became extinct shortly after human occupation and entire ecosystems collapsed. As wood could no longer be obtained, the islanders couldn't even build boats with which to escape and resorted to cannibalism to survive.

DID YOU KNOW?
The Polynesians are likely to have reached American shores long before the Vikings!

Polynesian boats had special storage areas in the hull so that belongings and livestock could be transported.

MOAI STATUES
More than 800 stupendous statues have been found on Easter Island (also known as 'Rapa Nui'). The enormous carvings were created in quarries, but many were transported several miles on wooden rollers and placed in formation.

Historians aren't quite sure what the statues represent, but many believe that the carvings were crafted to honour important chiefs.

Western Asia

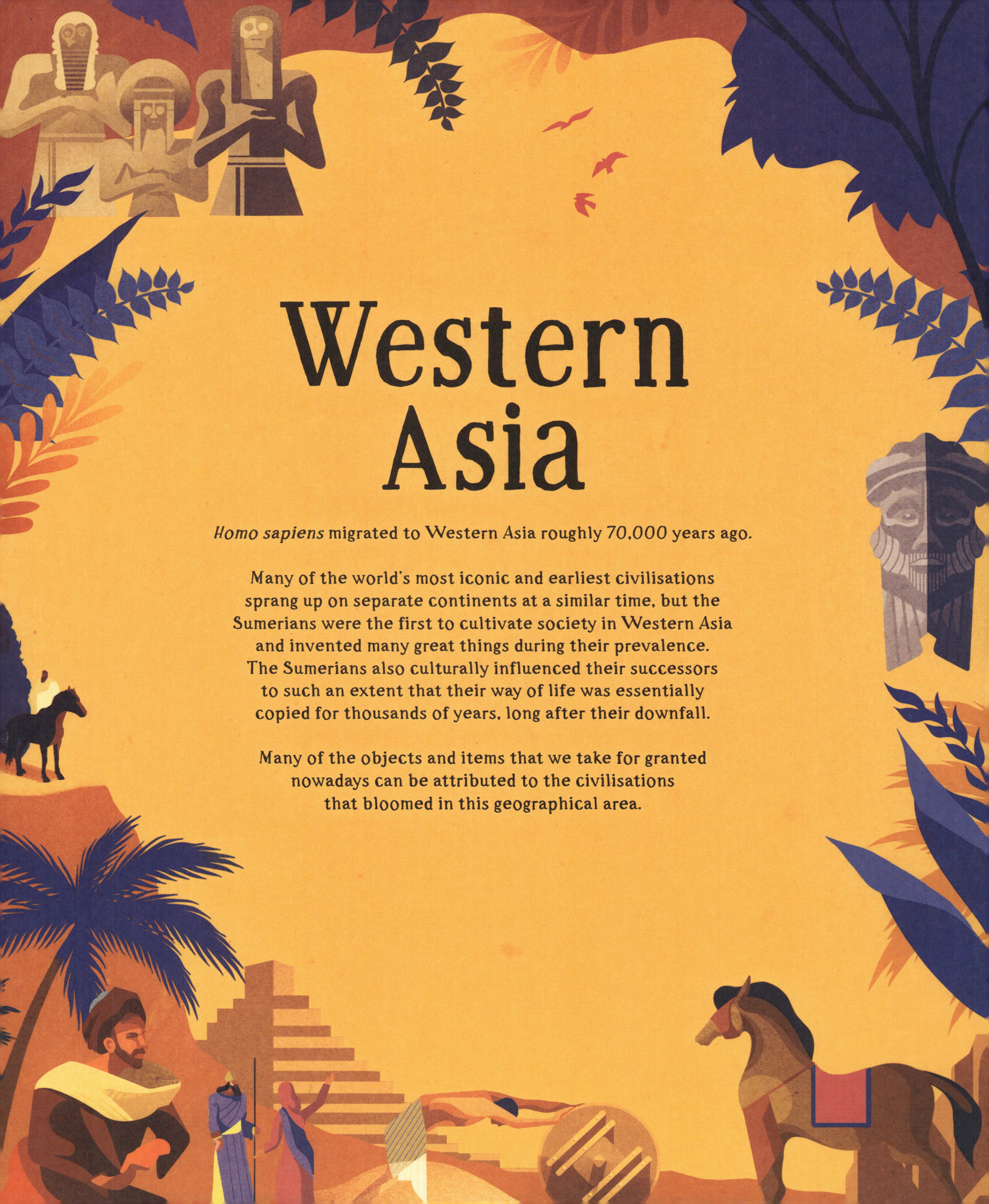

Homo sapiens migrated to Western Asia roughly 70,000 years ago.

Many of the world's most iconic and earliest civilisations sprang up on separate continents at a similar time, but the Sumerians were the first to cultivate society in Western Asia and invented many great things during their prevalence. The Sumerians also culturally influenced their successors to such an extent that their way of life was essentially copied for thousands of years, long after their downfall.

Many of the objects and items that we take for granted nowadays can be attributed to the civilisations that bloomed in this geographical area.

THE SUMERIANS

An ancient area known as Mesopotamia (meaning 'between two rivers' in Greek) is widely regarded as the birthplace of the first complex societies and civilisations. At its largest, Mesopotamia spanned hundreds of miles, covering Iraq and parts of modern day Iran, Syria and Turkey. The Sumerians created the first society here, rich in culture, wealth and language.

WHERE IN THE WORLD?

INCREDIBLE INVENTIONS

The Sumerians invented some astonishing things that helped shape human existence. We still use many of these technologies today:

THE (POTTER'S) WHEEL

The invention of the wheel revolutionised transport for humankind, and it is the Sumerians who are credited with its conception.

Though the wheel was originally used to turn clay into pots, vessels and vases, the Sumerians were the first to realise it could be placed vertically and used to roll heavy goods along the ground. Their descendants would eventually create chariots and wagons.

THE SAILBOAT

The Sumerians invented the sailboat, harnessing the power of the wind to help them transport goods and travel along two great rivers, the Tigris and Euphrates, or towards the sea. This greatly improved trade, allowing Sumerian merchants to travel against the river current and to meet people of different cultures.

THE SEED PLOUGH

Farming was vital for the Sumerians. The region they inhabited was predominantly semi-arid, and as more people spread across the land, farmers had to cultivate more crops to feed the booming population.

Farmers used the plough to cut channels and funnel seeds into the sun-baked surface of their soil, granting access to the more fertile and softer soil beneath. Planting seeds in these channels gave them a much better chance of growing. Sumerian farmers also dug a network of channels to transport river water towards their fields.

SCULPTURE AND CARVINGS

The Sumerians created beautiful sculptures and ornate carvings, often rendered from limestone, gypsum and a hard stone called diorite which was prized for its toughness. It would have taken Sumerian sculptors a long time to carve and chisel their statues and reliefs from such a solid stone, but some have stood the test of time and can be seen in museums today.

CLAY

Clay was used by humankind in approximately 25,000 BCE, but the Sumerians were the first to produce products from it on a truly grand scale, creating hundreds of thousands of clay tablets for inscribing; bricks for building; and pots, pans and other ceramics for daily use. For the Sumerians, clay provided a means of industry and was the foundation (quite literally) on which their civilisation was built.

CUNEIFORM SCRIPT

The Sumerians invented a sophisticated writing system, called cuneiform, which consisted of hundreds of characters and symbols.

But what did they do with all of these letters? Well, it looks as though the Sumerians were particularly fond of recording rather dull things on clay tablets, such as business transactions and deals! These tablets would be inscribed and then dried in the sun to create a permanent account.

Over time, cuneiform was adopted by more people and used for different purposes, like writing stories and laws. Cuneiform was so popular, in fact, that it was used as a form of communication for more than 3,000 years.

THE FIRST PERSON IN HISTORY

The invention of a written language allowed the Sumerians to create a record of history and the first human to be mentioned in written form was Kushim in around 3200 BCE. Kushim wasn't a divine ruler or a focal figure, but an accountant, and his signature at the bottom of a clay tablet is the first known of its kind.

The text on the tablet says:
29,086 MEASURES BARLEY
37 MONTHS
KUSHIM

BASE 60

We know that there are 60 seconds in a minute, 60 minutes in an hour, 24 hours in a day and 360 degrees in a full circle, but who came up with this radical way of thinking?

It was, in fact, the Sumerians. Their base-60 (sexagesimal) measurement system was adopted in the Mesopotamian region for centuries and is still used in some capacity today.

MONEY

Given that the Sumerians liked to record transactions and accounts, it makes perfect sense that they should also be the first in history to invent money, roughly 5,000 years ago. Goods, including metals, wool, oil and gems, were traded and used to barter and this system was supported by Sumerian currency, which didn't take the form of paper notes, but barley grains.

These grains were used as a benchmark against which to attribute value to almost everything, including food, drink, property, clothing, livestock and more. Wages were even paid in grain and money could literally be eaten! This form of currency was replaced several hundred years later when small measures of silver were introduced, called shekels.

THE AKKADIANS

The Akkadians, like the Sumerians, lived primarily in the region of Mesopotamia. In fact, the Akkadians and Sumerians were eventually governed as one people when war raged in 2334 BCE, creating what many historians deem the first empire.

The Akkadians laid the first foundations of a city that would eventually grow to become one of the biggest, most bustling and famous of ancient times – Babylon.

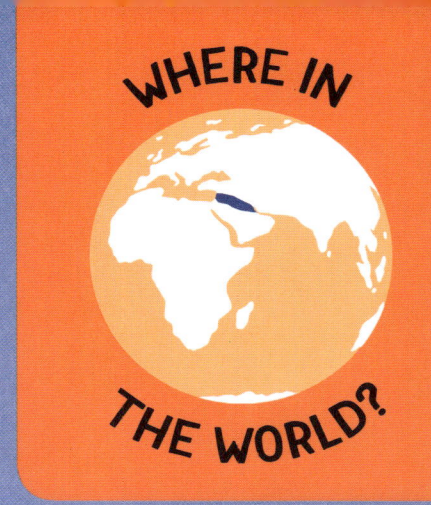

WHERE IN THE WORLD?

SARGON OF AKKAD

Sargon ruled for 56 years and helped unite the separate states in his kingdom, forming the world's first empire. He is rumoured to have been born into humble origins, possibly outcast at birth before being found by a lowly gardener. His mother was a priestess, but little is known about his father. He worked as a cupbearer in his youth, and rose to military prowess during a series of battles and invasions.

A bronze bust discovered in 1931, assumed to be a depiction of King Sargon.

LAMASSU

The Akkadians and Assyrians were renowned for building winged statues to ward off evil. The statues were usually placed near doorways or gates and were carved to look like lions or bulls, often with human heads.

ZIGGURATS

The people of Mesopotamia were famed for building enormous stepped pyramids called ziggurats. Some were more than 100m (330ft) wide and made from thousands of bricks. Each tier was thought to be adorned with trees and shrubs, creating lush gardens that could be enjoyed by its inhabitants. Many of the ziggurats from ancient times can be found in Iraq.

THE ASSYRIANS

The Assyrians are famous for creating some of the first literary works on clay tablets and for building on a grand scale. They recorded much of their history and military conquests by chiselling facts and stories into clay, many of which have been discovered by archaeologists. The remnants of some of the largest Assyrian cities can still be visited today at sites including Nineveh and Ashur in Iraq.

WHERE IN THE WORLD?

THE FIRST LIBRARY

King Ashurbanipal was passionate about the arts and built what many historians believe was the world's first library. Inscribers were sent to all corners of the empire to copy texts, including myths, prayers, stories and scientific works. At the point of Ashurbanipal's death, the library housed thousands of inscribed clay tablets, including *The Epic of Gilgamesh*.

FORGING

The Assyrians forged and smithed metals to use as tools, weapons and jewellery. Though tools had been wielded before, the Assyrians were the first to produce them at such speed and scale. Thanks to this, the Assyrian Empire expanded quickly. The opposition was simply no match for the well-equipped Assyrian soldiers.

THE EPIC OF GILGAMESH

The Epic of Gilgamesh is a 3,000 line poem that chronicles the adventures, trials and tribulations of a Sumerian king. The verse appears on a selection of clay tablets and the poem's protagonist is believed to be based on a real ruler of a city called Uruk, roughly 4,700 years ago.

The hero in the poem possesses super-human strength and is half-god, half-man. He has many dreams and nightmares during the course of the poem, and battles against a terrifying forest guardian called Humbaba in his quest for immortality. Despite obtaining a special life-giving plant from the bottom of the sea and staying awake for as long as he can, Gilgamesh's fight for eternal life is fruitless and he faces the stark realisation that he will one day die. He finally returns to Uruk where he praises the work of the gods.

HUMBABA'S HEAD

GILGAMESH

THE BABYLONIANS

The first mention of Babylon dates back to the third millenium BCE, but the city didn't truly prosper until the reign of King Hammurabi during the First Babylonian Dynasty (1792-1750 BCE) when Babylon became the epicentre of the Babylonian Empire and home to an estimated 200,000 people. The Babylonians fell in and out of power during the next 1,100 years, eventually forming the Neo-Babylonian society in the 7th and 6th centuries BCE, when the once-great city thrived again…

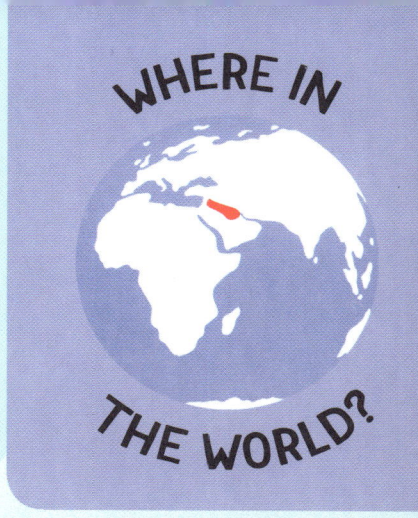

WHERE IN THE WORLD?

BABYLON

Babylon's foundations were laid approximately 4,000 years ago and the city was ruled by several peoples during its existence. The metropolis thrived until 539 BCE when it was sacked and razed by the Persian army, signifying the end of the Mesopotamian Empire.

Babylon was one of the largest cities of ancient times, famed for housing one of the world's Seven Wonders – the Hanging Gardens. According to ancient script, King Nebuchadnezzar II built the Hanging Gardens because his wife, Amytis of Media, pined for the lush vegetation and flowers of her homeland. Nebuchadnezzar created a verdant garden in which she could wander.

THE CODE OF HAMMURABI

Hammurabi was an ancient king who founded the city of Babylon. He was the first figure to create a written code of ethics and rules for his people to obey, implementing punishments for rule-breaking citizens, including monetary fines and physical punishments. People could even be sentenced to death!

Though Hammurabi's code was groundbreaking for society at the time, the rules and codes may now seem quite barbaric. His laws weren't very fair either, as people from lower classes received different (often harsher) treatment to the upper classes.

THE PERSIANS

The Persian Empire spread widely and rapidly, perhaps more swiftly than any other civilisation in history, engulfing parts of India in the East and Europe in the West within just two centuries. The Persians conquered much of Eurasia, but eventually stumbled when attempting to invade Greece, famously losing much of their navy to the Athenians.

The Persians are often vilified in the history books for being tyrannical warmongers, but there was certainly much more to their civilisation than meets the eye.

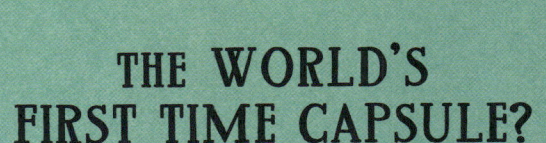

WHERE IN THE WORLD?

THE WORLD'S FIRST TIME CAPSULE?

The Persians created the Cyrus Cylinder in the 6th century BCE. The 20cm- (8in-) long clay baton is inscribed with one of the first human-rights declarations concerning rights and ethics. It states that Cyrus the Great, with the help of the god, Marduk, captured Babylon and freed its inhabitants and slaves from bondage and tyranny. The cylinder was transcribed in 539 BCE and concealed within the city walls, acting like a time capsule until its discovery, almost 2,500 years later.

THE POSTAL SERVICE

Evidence of the first postal service is said to date back 2,500 years to the Achaemenid Persian Empire, ruled by Cyrus the Great.

The Persian kingdom became so vast and militant that it required an advanced messaging system. It was vital that important news and battle commands be relayed, so horseriders were employed to travel day and night in order to transfer these messages. Post offices were strategically placed no further than a day's ride from each other. This meant that letters could be passed as quickly as possible with no time wasted.

FRIDGES

The Persians are thought to have built the first *yakhchāl* (fridges) in approximatley 400 BCE. Unlike the buzzing refrigerators of today, which guzzle electricity and gas, the Persians collected ice from parts of their kingdom to be piled in a domed vessel, insulated with a special type of building material called *sārooj*. These vessels channelled cold air and cool water to keep ice frozen, even in warmer weather.

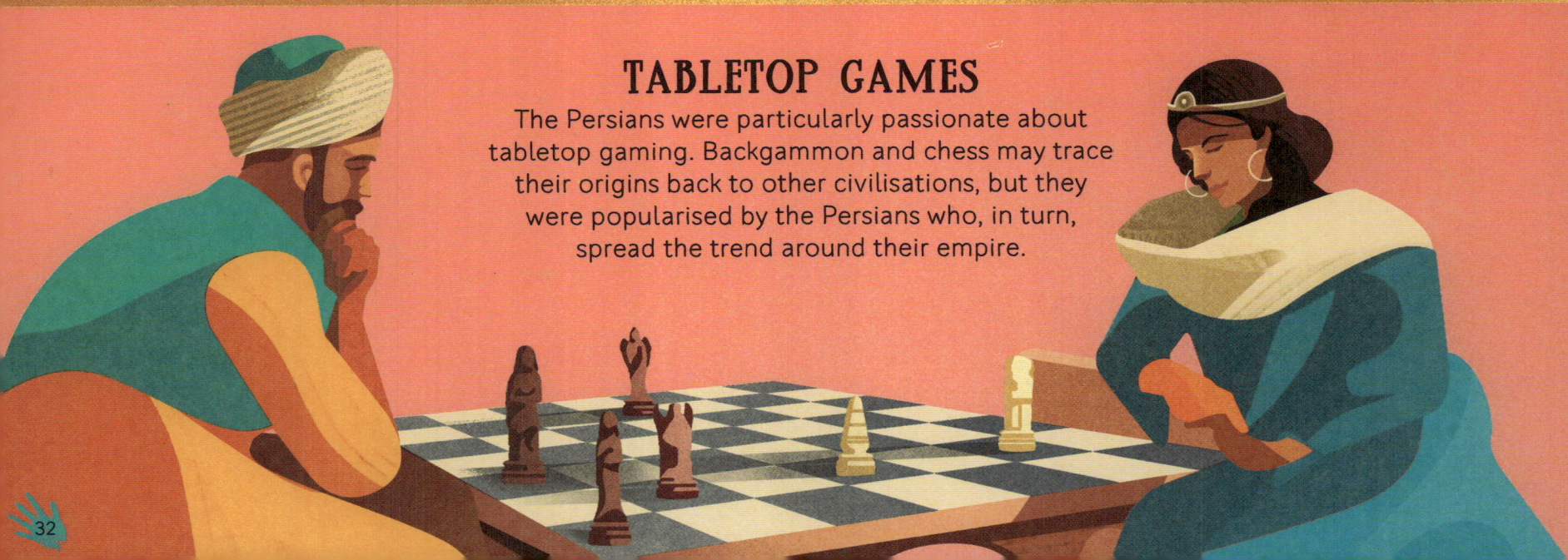

TABLETOP GAMES

The Persians were particularly passionate about tabletop gaming. Backgammon and chess may trace their origins back to other civilisations, but they were popularised by the Persians who, in turn, spread the trend around their empire.

Eastern Asia

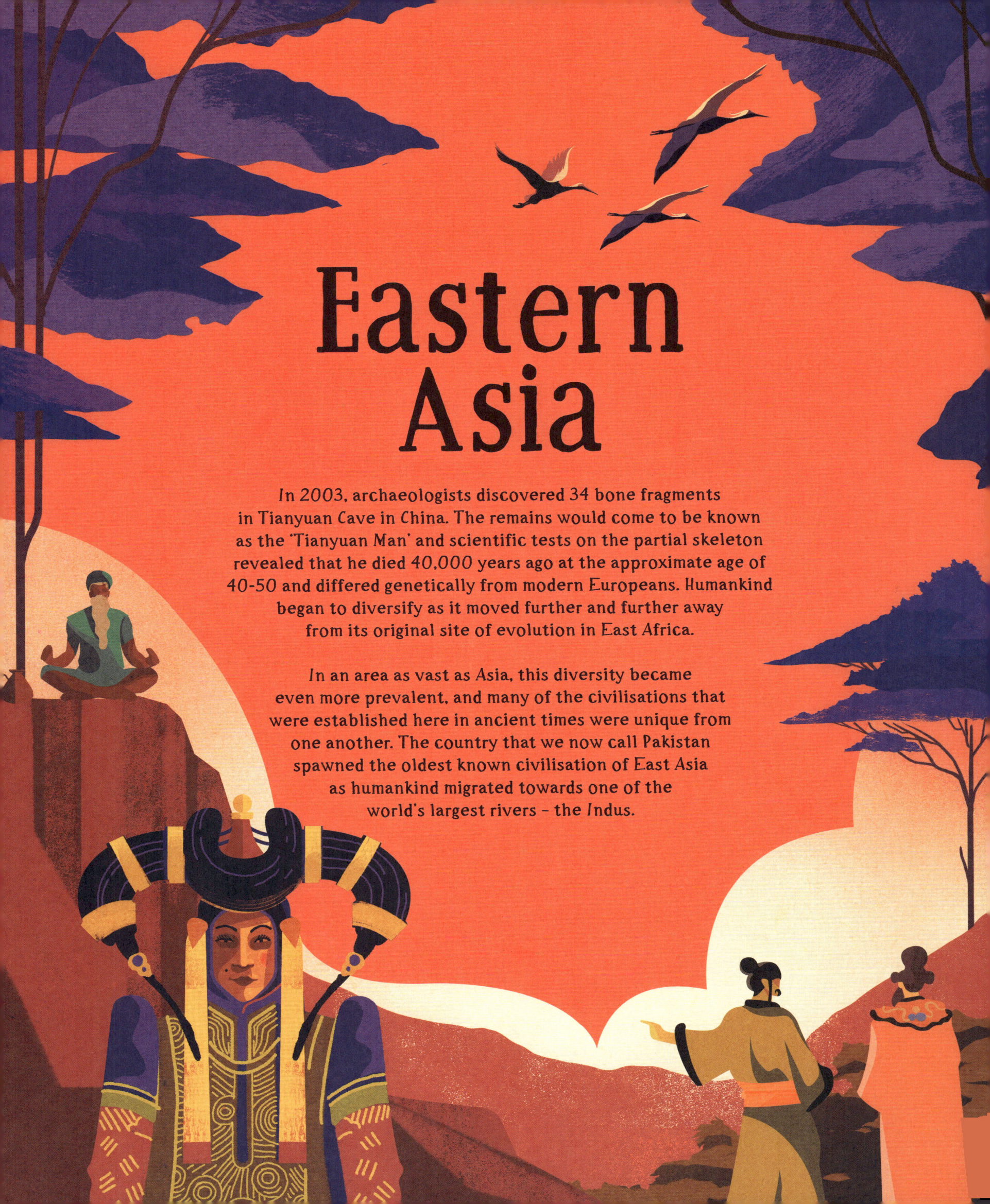

In 2003, archaeologists discovered 34 bone fragments in Tianyuan Cave in China. The remains would come to be known as the 'Tianyuan Man' and scientific tests on the partial skeleton revealed that he died 40,000 years ago at the approximate age of 40-50 and differed genetically from modern Europeans. Humankind began to diversify as it moved further and further away from its original site of evolution in East Africa.

In an area as vast as Asia, this diversity became even more prevalent, and many of the civilisations that were established here in ancient times were unique from one another. The country that we now call Pakistan spawned the oldest known civilisation of East Asia as humankind migrated towards one of the world's largest rivers – the Indus.

THE PEOPLE OF THE INDUS VALLEY

WHERE IN THE WORLD?

About 5,000 years ago, an influx of people settled beside the banks of the Indus River – the longest river in modern-day Pakistan. Using the river water and the flooded plains, they created thriving farming communities, eventually flocking towards a fertile area known as the Indus Valley, cultivating a civilisation that would exist for 1,500 years.

At its largest, the Indus civilisation stretched some 250,000 square miles, all the way from Pakistan to India, making it much larger than the Egyptian and Mesopotamian civilisations that preceded it.

The source of the Indus River begins in the Himalayas, winding around monumental mountains, cascading through dense jungle and curving towards the Arabian Sea.

AN UNCRACKABLE CODE

Modern-day linguists haven't been able to decipher the written language used by the Indus people and, as a result, we still don't know much about their way of life. More than 400 symbols or characters have been compiled by archaeologists, but not enough material has been found to fill in the gaps.

Unlike the Egyptians and Mesopotamians, it is possible that the Indus people inscribed their words on leaves or wooden boards or panels which have long since perished. Historians aren't even sure what caused the civilisation to capitulate.

WEIGHTS AND MEASURES

The first ruler in history was found in the Indus Valley and this culture produced some of the first measures of weight.

DRAINS AND TOILETS

Though the Romans are often considered to be the leading architects and engineers of the ancient world, the people of the Indus Valley were the first to properly plan their towns, introducing grid systems, bath houses and drainage systems. It is thought that even the most basic of houses had a means of flushing waste and that streets had covered drains. Most of the Indus towns and cities were also protected by flood defences.

The buildings and structures in this area were created almost exclusively from bricks and many of their ruins can still be seen today.

DID YOU KNOW?

The practice of meditation may be more than 5,000 years old. Archaeologists discovered murals in the Indus Valley depicting people in meditative poses.

BUTTONS

Buttons were first made from sea shells more than 4,500 years ago. Though we now use buttons to fasten items of clothing, the people of the Indus Valley used them for decorative purposes, carving geometric designs into the shells before stitching them on to garments.

THE ANCIENT CHINESE

China was governed by many rulers and families during ancient times and 'dynasties' were established, whereby leadership was passed from one generation to another. The time of the Han Dynasty (206 BCE–220 CE) was a particularly pivotal era, amid which many existing cultural practices were first introduced.

WHERE IN THE WORLD?

TEA
Aside from water, tea is the most popular drink in the world and it was first created by the Chinese.

DID YOU KNOW?
In 1971, construction workers found the Lady of Dai, a 2,000-year-old mummy dating back to the Han Dynasty. The mummy was so well preserved that some of her blood vessels were intact.

THE SILK ROAD
The Silk Road was a pivotal trading route between parts of Africa and Europe in the West and India and China in the East. The Chinese network of pathways was established during the Han period.

PAPER
Cai Lun is thought to have invented paper from the bark of a mulberry tree in 105 CE. Archaeological evidence shows that paper was in existence before this time, but it was Cai Lun's apprentice who ensured the growth of its popularity throughout China. The production of paper also led to the creation of bank notes for the first time.

GREAT WALL OF CHINA
The Great Wall of China is the longest man-made structure in the world. It was built to protect the country from invading hordes and stretches, weaves and winds a staggering 21,196km (13,170mi) through rugged terrain. The wall was developed over the course of several centuries by different Chinese tribes and leaders. Many clans created walls to protect themselves in the 7th and 8th centuries BCE, and Qin Shi Huang, the first Chinese emperor, started connecting the ramparts to create a solid wall in the 3rd century BCE.

CONFUCIUS

Confucius was a teacher and philosopher. His work argued that individuals should treat each other the way they would want to be treated, and focussed on the importance of family and education. A classical Chinese education was quite different from the curriculum now taught in schools - pupils studied archery, calligraphy, mathematics, music, chariot-driving and ritual as their core subjects.

CONFUCIUS

UMBRELLAS

China can experience some severe weather patterns and the umbrella was originally used to shield the rich from blistering sunshine.

The Romans, on the other hand, used umbrellas to protect against heavy downpours.

THE SEISMOSCOPE

During the Han Dynasty (206 BCE – 220 CE) there were many technological advances, one of which was the invention of the seismoscope – an instrument used to detect earthquakes. Invented by a mighty mathematician called Zhang Heng in 132 CE, the contraption was adorned with eight dragon heads and eight gulping frogs. Whenever there was a tremor, the dragons dropped balls into the frogs' mouths, creating an alarm signal.

EDUCATION

Under Emperor Wudi's guidance, scholars Gongsun Hong and Dong Zhongshu established the first imperial university called the Taixue during the Han Dynasty.

Education became increasingly important as it allowed people to switch ranks in a structured society. Pupils who passed their final year exams at university would be selected for employment in the civil service. This allowed society to progress based on intellect and ability, rather than wealth.

Gongsun Hong was one of Emperor Wudi's most trusted advisors, yet he came from humble beginnings and was a pig farmer until he started studying Confucian texts at the age of 40.

DID YOU KNOW?
In the 9th century CE, Chinese alchemists accidentally concocted gunpowder when attempting to create a medicine that could grant longer life.

DID YOU KNOW?
Ching Shih, an 18th century pirate, commanded a huge naval force known as the Red Flag Fleet. Historians think this may have been the largest force of pirates in history, consisting of several hundred ships and up to 50,000 buccaneers.

Ching Shih was a ruthless leader and she kept her motley crew in check with some strict rules; most crimes were punishable by beheading. Ching Shih was feared to such an extent that the government eventually offered her a pardon. After attacking several towns and cities, she retired to live a quieter life in the country.

THE MONGOLS

The Mongol Empire was one of the largest ever to exist, shrouding almost all of Asia and a large chunk of the European continent. Founded by Genghis Khan in 1206, the kingdom rapidly expanded over the course of the century but wars with factions in China and the spread of the Black Death (plague) during the 1300s sparked its slow decline.

WHERE IN THE WORLD?

GENGHIS KHAN

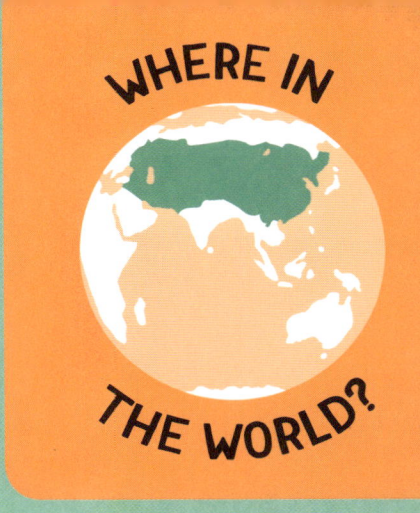

During the late 12th century, a series of skirmishes and inter-tribal battles erupted among the Mongolian people. By 1206, however, Genghis Khan had unified the Mongolian tribes and wiped out the competition to become the country's sole ruler. With a vast army at his back, Genghis then began to expand the empire, invading China before heading west and northwards into Russia.

Genghis brought great prosperity to his people, but his armies and generals also inflicted plenty of violence under his command. After his death, Genghis Khan's bloodline continued to expand the empire. His grandson, Kublai, even conquered the rest of China, becoming emperor and the first Mongol to rule over the entire country!

By 1227 CE
By 1279 CE

DID YOU KNOW?
So far-reaching was the Mongol Empire that every 1 in 200 men alive today is a relative of Genghis Khan!

DID YOU KNOW?
Genghis Khan (1162 – 1227 CE) was rumoured to have been holding a blood clot in his hand when he was born!

The Mongol Empire covered more than 9 million square miles (roughly 16% of the planet's land) and encapsulated approximately 25% of the planet's population at the time.

WHAT ABOUT THE REST OF ASIA?

Asia is the largest continent on Earth, so it should come as no surprise that its history is rich with culture. Enormous sprawling civilisations dominated this humongous region, but many peoples and ethnic groups formed their own kingdoms across these vast lands.

MAURYANS

When Alexander the Great removed troops from regions in India in 321 BCE, Chandragupta Maurya seized power by uniting the Indian states. At its peak, the Mauryan army was said to have had more than 600,000 soldiers and 9,000 war elephants!

THE KHMER

The Khmer people established their capital city of Angkor in Cambodia and many of the ornately carved temple complexes can be seen today, including Angkor Wat and Bayon. The Khmer language is still spoken in Cambodia and the ornate stupas of Angkor Wat are featured on the national flag.

THE HUNS

The Hunnic civilisation is widely regarded as history's most bloodthirsty! Under the rule of Attila, a despotic leader who killed his own brother in 445 CE, the Huns invaded much of Europe, battling against a declining Roman Empire. Attila himself died on his wedding night under mysterious circumstances!

DID YOU KNOW?
The temples at Angkor are spread over land as vast as 150 football pitches, making it the largest religious site in the world.

RELIGION
All of the world's major or classic religions hail from Asia: Baháʼí, Buddhism, Christianity, Confucianism, Hinduism, Islam, Jainism, Judaism, Shinto, Sikhism, Taoism and Zoroastrianism.

Europe

Plenty of Stone, Bronze and Iron Age settlements are scattered across the European continent, and ruins can be found in places as remote as Orkney on the northeastern tip of Scotland.

The oldest-known European civilisation, however, belonged to the Minoans of the Bronze Age, who governed their kingdom from the island of Crete. Their artistic lifestyle influenced many other peoples including the ancient Greeks and Romans, with the Roman Empire being widely regarded as the most successful in history thanks to its military prowess.

THE MINOANS

The roots of the Minoan civilisation can be traced back to the island of Crete in the Aegean (Mediterranean) Sea. Settlers may have sailed to the island from as early as 7000 BCE and a Bronze Age kingdom was established here in approximately 3000 BCE, creating a culture that would prevail for 2,000 years and spread across much of the Mediterranean.

WHERE IN THE WORLD?

THE MINOTAUR

DID YOU KNOW?

Knossos is one of Europe's oldest cities and the setting for one of history's finest myths. According to legend, a beast called the Minotaur was imprisoned deep within an inescapable maze buried beneath the palace.

The Minotaur had the body of a man and the head of a bull and ate human flesh! Theseus, one of many Greek heroes, eventually slew the beast and navigated his way back through the maze using a spool of thread.

ARTS AND CRAFTS

The Minoan civilisation is lauded for its sophisticated art and crafts culture. The first frescoes (wall paintings brushed on to wet plaster) were created by the Minoans and many of the first mosaics can still be seen in the palace at Knossos and in Heraklion Architectural Museum.

THE ANCIENT GREEKS

From the dramatic genre of tragedy to the mathematical field of geometry, ancient Greece is famous for its intellectual achievements. The civilisation began in around 800 BCE and by 323 BCE, Alexander the Great had explored and invaded lands as far away as northern India. At the end of the Hellenistic period (31 BCE), ancient Greeks could come from places as diverse as Ionia (Turkey), Egypt and Parthia (Afghanistan).

WHERE IN THE WORLD?

GREEK MYTH

The Greeks believed in many gods and goddesses and the tales attributed to their deities are now retold as myths. There were 12 major gods, known as Olympians, and they ruled from atop Mount Olympus.

Ancient Greeks were fond of sublime stories embellished by imagination and their myths are full of menacing beasts, including the snake-haired gorgons, fire-breathing Chimera and many more ...

LERNAEAN HYDRA

The Hydra had nine heads, and for every head that was severed, another would grow in its place.

Heracles and his nephew, Iolaus, defeated the Hydra for his second labour.

DID YOU KNOW?

Zeus was the king of the gods, and Hera was the queen. Together, they governed the other Olympian deities: Aphrodite, Apollo, Ares, Artemis, Athena, Demeter, Dionysus, Hephaestus, Hermes and Poseidon.

HERACLES

Heracles, also known as Hercules in Roman myth, was a Greek hero. He completed 12 labours (challenges) set by an evil ruler called King Eurystheus.

PHILOSOPHY

Philosophy, meaning 'love of wisdom' in ancient Greek, is the study of knowledge, behaviour and existence. The ancient Greeks were philosophic pioneers and they founded many principles that we still learn today.

LITERATURE

The ancient Greek civilisation produced plenty of talented wordsmiths, many works of which are still in print today and often studied in schools, colleges and universities!

SOCRATES

Socrates, a renowned philosopher, is famous for his use of questions to break down accepted ways of thinking. Although none of Socrates' writing now exists, his follower Plato wrote an awful lot about his methods! Socrates' teachings inspired many great minds including Aristotle and Alexander the Great.

SAPPHO

Sappho was a Greek poet born in the 7th century BCE. She was considered to be one of the most talented writers of her time. Coins were minted with her face imprinted on them, proving just how well-respected she was. Unfortunately, just one of Sappho's complete poems exists today and everything else we know about her writings has been gleaned from fragments of texts and quotes from other authors.

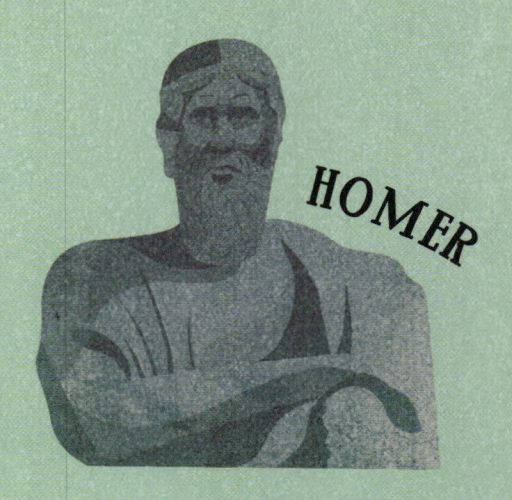

HYPATIA

Hypatia was an immensely talented philosopher and astronomer and one of the world's greatest mathematicians. She was born in 355 BCE in the city of Alexandria, Egypt, during a particularly tumultuous period when the area was governed by the ancient Greeks. Religious uprisings in this region eventually reached fever pitch and Hypatia herself was murdered by Christian fanatics.

HOMER

Homer's *Iliad* and *Odyssey* are the most famous ancient Greek poems. They are oral epics, originally spoken, rather than written down. *The Iliad* is set during the Trojan War, a mythical clash between Troy and Greece.

The Odyssey details the homeward journey of the Greek hero Odysseus. During this perilous voyage, he encounters many mythical characters and monsters.

DID YOU KNOW?

Spiky dog collars were invented by the ancient Greeks. As the Greek empire expanded, soldiers and travellers began to notice that their dogs weren't returning from hunts...

The Greeks had encroached on lion and wolf territory! So owners started fitting the dogs with spiky collars. Lions and wolves often kill by chomping at the throat of their prey and this invention acted as a deterrent.

DID YOU KNOW?

One of the most famous cities Alexander the Great founded was Alexandria in Egypt. It was home to the legendary Alexandrian library, which was supposedly filled with every Greek text and with writings from across the world.

OLYMPIC GAMES

The ancient Greeks were fond of sport and created the Olympic Games in approximately 776 BCE. Sprinting was the only sporting event featured at the first games, and other disciplines, including wrestling, boxing, javelin, discus and long jump, were added as the years went by.

The modern Olympic Games began in 1896 and nowadays athletes from more than 200 countries take part.

THE ROMANS

Starting as a collection of thatched huts on the Palatine Hill between the 10th and 9th century BCE, Rome spawned an empire that encompassed the Mediterranean, Middle East and large areas of Europe and northern Africa. Most of these places were conquered while Rome was a republic and the empire reached its greatest size during the time of Emperor Hadrian who ruled from 117-138 CE.

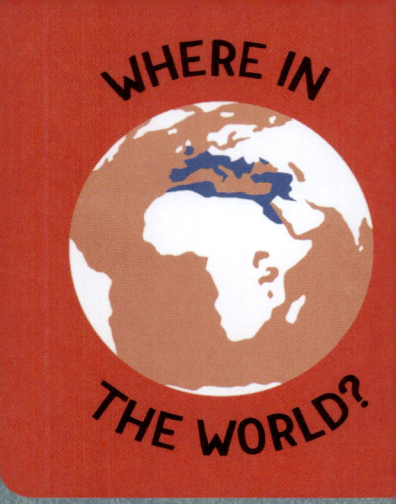

WHERE IN THE WORLD?

POWER TO THE PEOPLE

Between 509 BCE and 27 BCE, Rome existed as a republic – this meant that the Senate (council) held power and made decisions for the state. At first, only patricians (the landowning, aristocratic class) could become senators and this created tension with the plebeians (other citizens). In 366 BCE, a plebeian council was founded to try and balance the power dynamics.

During Roman supremacy, many political figures, activists and slaves stood up for social reform! The balance of power shifted slightly during this time and the people collectively held more power.

HORTENSIA

Hortensia was a famous orator (public speaker). She spoke out against a tax on 1,400 women to raise military funds. Hortensia argued that women should not pay for civil wars in which they did not participate.

The number of women taxed was reduced to 400 and a similar levy was created for men as a result of Hortensia's campaign.

JULIUS CAESAR

Julius Caesar was a Roman general and politician who seized power and leadership of Rome, partly due to the military prowess he showed when conquering the province of Gaul (France).

On returning to Italy after his conquests, Caesar refused to follow orders to give up military command, prompting a vicious civil war with a politician called Pompey, a former ally. Despite having a smaller army, Caesar defeated Pompey decisively at the Battle of Pharsalus in Greece in 48 BCE.

Caesar became a permanent 'dictator' of Rome. Some senators were afraid that one man holding so much power would destroy the Roman Republic and secretly plotted to have him killed. Led by Cassius and Brutus, the assailants assassinated Caesar in 44 BCE. Ironically, the battles and riots that followed cemented the power of Caesar's adopted son, Octavian, who became the first emperor of Rome.

THE JULIAN CALENDAR

At the advice of Alexandrian astronomer Sosigenes, Caesar created a 12-month solar calendar of 365 days. This calendar is very similar to the one we use today.

ARE YOU NOT ENTERTAINED?

Spartacus was a Roman soldier, but he deserted his duties and was eventually captured and sold as a slave. In 73 BCE, he escaped from a gladiatorial training camp, joining other runaways on the slopes of Mount Vesuvius. As many as 90,000 rebels are said to have banded together, fighting off the Roman army whenever it attacked.

Spartacus, along with the majority of his supporters, eventually perished in battle, but his legacy helped empower the slaves. As a result of this war, slave-owners and leaders alike were more cautious in their treatment of enslaved men and women.

BUILDING AN EMPIRE

The Romans revolutionised architecture and engineering by creating new building techniques, using different materials and designing cutting-edge technologies.

FAST FOOD

All the building and fighting was tiresome and, as the empire expanded, more mouths needed to be fed. Fast food became particularly popular at this time as busy people were constantly on the move.

Burgers, chips and hotdogs weren't on the menu, but dormice covered in honey may have been!

CONCRETE

Concrete may have existed since 3000 BCE, but Roman concrete followed a far superior recipe and many of the structures built with this unique concoction have withstood the test of time – even piers and coastal constructions. The mixture of volcanic ash, lime (calcium oxide), seawater and chunks of volcanic rock has been lauded by scientists for its ability to get stronger, not weaker, as the years go by!

ROADS

The army played a pivotal role in the expansion of the Roman Empire. It was so important, in fact, that engineers built straight roads to help transport soldiers around the empire as quickly and efficiently as possible!

HEATING SYSTEMS

The Romans famously built underfloor heating systems, called hypocausts, to warm their bath houses. Furnaces were constructed and lit beneath ground and the hot air was then channelled through openings to create a central heating system and a means of warming pools to different temperatures. The wealthy eventually incorporated this technology for use in the home during the cold winter months.

THE CELTS

The Celts spanned much of Europe between 700 BCE and the 1st century CE, settling in regions of Spain, Ireland, France, Romania, Austria, Germany and the British Isles to name a few. As the Roman Empire expanded, the two peoples (Celts and Romans) clashed and the factions were often at war with one another.

WHERE IN THE WORLD?

DID YOU KNOW?
When walking into battle, the Celts allegedly liked to paint their naked bodies with patterns and designs in order to communicate with their gods and to strike fear into their enemies. Unfortunately, their nakedness was often no match for the heavily armoured Roman soldiers they fought against!

QUEEN BOUDICCA
Queen Boudicca belonged to the Iceni tribe in an area of England now known as Norfolk. She led a revolt against the Romans in 60 CE, after her husband's kingdom was unfairly plundered and divided rather than inherited by the leading tribesfolk, or by Boudicca and her daughters.

Boudicca formed an alliance with neighbouring tribes and marched on Camulodunum (Colchester), the Roman capital city of England, burning it to the ground, before turning her attention to Verulamium (St Albans) and Londinium (London). The battles were particularly bloody and the Celts killed more than 70,000 Romans by the time the rebellion was quashed. Boudicca's forces were eventually defeated by Suetonius Paulinus and the Roman legions.

The cause of Boudicca's death is unclear, but it is likely that she took poison or died from an ailment linked to stress and exhaustion. Boudicca's rebellion may have inflicted the first crack in the foundation of the Roman Empire, but it would take another three centuries for the Romans to withdraw their forces from the British Isles.

DID YOU KNOW?
Each Celtic clan had its own leader. In England, alone, there were more than 30 distinct tribes, each with a unique dialect. Some Celtic languages still exist today, including Gaelic, Manx and Welsh.

THE VIKINGS

The Vikings hailed from Denmark, Norway and Sweden in the Scandinavian region of Europe and created small farming communities and fishing villages, rather than sprawling cities, throughout their lands.

Many Vikings began to leave their homeland towards the end of the 8th century (CE), sailing to France, Ireland and Scotland, probably as a result of waning resources. The Vikings developed their own unique culture and sailed to islands and areas in the Atlantic Ocean that had never before been visited by Europeans.

COMBS

Viking men and women alike are often depicted with long, luscious locks of hair. Why would this be?

Well ... archaeologists have unearthed plenty of examples of Viking combs, many of which are intricately carved from deer antlers. Historians believe that warriors may have even carried combs on their belts and that grooming was an integral part of Viking culture.

WHERE IN THE WORLD?

DID YOU KNOW?
The Vikings were originally referred to as Danes, long before the country of Denmark was given its name.

EXPLORATION

The Scandinavian landscape is rich in a mineral called magnetite, which is known for its magnetic properties. The Vikings were rumoured to have been the first to harness its qualities by creating compasses, enabling them to navigate great distances.

The Viking Empire used Iceland as its primary naval hub, launching ships across the Atlantic Ocean in order to expand its territories. Erik the Red is said to have been the first European to discover Greenland in the 10th century and his son, Leif, travelled all the way to North American shores at the turn of the 11th century. Erik created his very own Viking colony in Greenland, but Leif and his men were forced from Canadian lands when they were attacked by natives.

GLASSES

Many peoples in history lay claim to the invention of spectacles. The Vikings have a strong claim, as archaeological exploration of the Swedish town of Fröjel in 1999 uncovered crystal lenses almost 1,000 years old.

SKIS

Ancient cave paintings suggest that the first skis may have been fashioned more than 20,000 years ago in Asia, but it was the Vikings who tinkered with the design and used them on a regular basis. Skis help spread their user's weight over a larger surface area and were used as a safe means of travel over the ice and soft snow abundant in Scandinavia.

The Americas

Once our ancient ancestors had explored and traversed the huge expanse of the Eurasian landmass, travelling further northwards and eastwards over the course of several millennia, they eventually reached North America in approximately 11,000 BCE. The land between western Canada and eastern Russia is still linked today by the Bering Strait, but the pathway has long since been submerged by rising sea levels.

The harsh conditions and subzero temperatures of the north probably prompted humans to travel rapidly towards the warmer climes of Central and South America shortly after their arrival. It is suspected that humans had settled in South America by 10,000 BCE, and that waves of people may have spanned the entire length and breadth of the Americas in as little as 4,000 years.

THE NATIVE AMERICANS

Humans entered North America from the north-eastern tip of what we now call Russia roughly 13,000 years ago, forming tribes and settlements as they explored the vast country. Some of these peoples are extant today, including the Apache, Cherokee and Cheyenne. Much like the Aboriginal Australians, Native Americans lived in isolation for thousands of years, helping to preserve their culturally rich way of life.

WHERE IN THE WORLD?

TRANSPORT IN TOUGH CONDITIONS

The tip of the North American continent is famed for its rugged conditions and ice-cold climate. The Native Americans had to come up with some nifty methods of transportation to tackle these harsh conditions:

KAYAKS

The Inuit, Yup'ik and Aleut peoples of North America invented kayaks, which were originally made from wood, animal skins and whale blubber.

Most Native American tribes settled close to water for sustenance and relied on fish as a staple food source. The kayak allowed hunters to fish in deeper waters, and to travel across lakes and along meltwater and rivers.

TOBOGGANS

Invented by the Anishinaabe people of the North American continent, toboggans, also called sledges, could be dragged, pushed or ridden over icy and snowy ground. The Native Americans would have used them to transport heavy goods over long distances rather than to slide down steep hills for fun!

53

LACROSSE

The origins of lacrosse can be traced all the way back to the Algonquian people, who originally named the game 'stickball'. The sport evolved over the centuries. Originally, matches could last several days, goals could be miles apart and players could number in their thousands! There were also very few rules! Lacrosse wasn't just for warriors, either, and was played by people from many different tribes.

Today, lacrosse is played around the world, though players are limited to ten per team. The US and Canadian teams are the only nations to have won the World Lacrosse Championships.

DID YOU KNOW?
During the 18th and 19th centuries, many nations fought for control of North American land, including Britain, France, Russia and Spain. The Native Americans were unjustly forced from their territories as a result of European conquest and expanding empires.

THE DISCOVERY OF OIL
Oil is a worldwide energy source and most of us rely on it to power our machines, vehicles and contraptions on a daily basis, but when was it discovered?

Many ancient civilisations used oil as a flammable source of light and its by-products (asphalt and bitumen) to seal and waterproof their ships and to stick things together. Edwin Drake, an American businessman, was the first person to successfully 'strike' oil in Pennsylvania, USA, in 1859, but Native Americans had long since attributed a value to the flammable liquid.

In fact, more than 400 years earlier, the Iroquois people dug pits in Pennsylvania in order to extract oil, using it as bug repellant and for medicinal purposes. The Iroquois dug to depths of up to 6m (20ft). It would have taken days, if not weeks, to reach such distances, proving just how important the Native Americans considered oil to be.

MEDICINE

Native Americans harvested thousands of different plants for their medicinal qualities, including rosemary, coca and devil's claw.

Some Inuits still live in Russia today, but many are from Alaska, Canada and Greenland.

The Paleo-Inuit people travelled from Asia into North America roughly 6,000 years ago.

TEEPEES

As the Native Americans ventured further into the Americas, shelter became problematic. How could a nomadic people protect itself from the cold winds and plummeting temperatures without portable housing? The teepee provided the answer.

Made from sticks and animal skins, the shelter could be erected and dismantled with relative ease and transported between campsites. This incredible invention inspired the design for modern-day tents.

THE OLMECS

The Olmec civilisation emerged more than 3,500 years ago and controlled much of Mesoamerica from approximately 1200 BCE – 400 BCE. It was the first major empire in this region and many of the Olmec practices, technologies and teachings were adopted by the Maya and Aztecs.

WHERE IN THE WORLD?

CHOCOLATE

The Olmecs are recognised as being the first to harvest, grind and roast cacao beans in order to create a popular bitter-tasting drink circa 1500 BCE. This recipe was passed from generation to generation and the beverage was infused with herbs and spices for different occasions. When sweet-toothed Europeans invaded in the 16th century and discovered the recipe for themselves, they began to add sugar. Drinking chocolate soon became popular as a sweet treat across the continent.

Chocolate as we know it today has only existed for a few centuries and the first chocolate bar wasn't made until 1847.

RUBBER

The Olmec people harvested a milky liquid called latex from trees and plants more than 3,000 years ago and combined it with juice from other flowering plants to make rubber. Ingredients were then added in different quantities to produce rubber that was hard or soft – excellent for ball games!

DID YOU KNOW?
Cacao beans were particularly valuable in ancient times and were used as a currency by Mesoamerican peoples. According to an Aztec text, 100 beans could be traded for one turkey.

THE MAYA

Unlike many civilisations, the Maya did not build an ever-expanding empire but existed as a collection of city-states with a shared culture and religious system.

This civilisation flourished between 300 CE and 900 CE and its sophisticated cities, some of which can still be seen today, demonstrate just how advanced the Maya were in their astounding understanding of astronomy and mathematics. Maya people continue to live in some rural Central-American communities.

MATHEMATICS

To help them with their astronomical calculations, the Maya had an elegant mathematical system with three symbols: a shell for zero, a dot for one and a bar for five.

TIME

The Maya followed both a 260-day ritual calendar and a 365-day solar calendar which was divided into 18 months of 20 days.

Wait ...
18 x 20 = 360 ...

So what did the Maya do with the remaining five days? Well, they were considered to be very unlucky and the Maya spent those ominous hours praying to the gods.

One of the reasons keeping time was so important to the Maya was because different time periods were considered to be gods in their own right and time itself was worshipped.

WHAT IS A CITY STATE?

City states govern their own affairs and are independent of the country or territory surrounding them. City states have existed for an incredibly long time, and modern examples include Monaco, Vatican City and Singapore.

WHERE IN THE WORLD?

ASTRONOMY

The Maya were obsessed with the movements of the planets. So much so that they built certain cities and structures to align with celestial bodies.

The Maya plotted the positions of the Sun, Moon and Venus, and also predicted eclipses. There is even archaeological evidence suggesting that Mayan astronomers worked out the timing it takes the Earth to orbit the Sun with such accuracy that their calculations are not too dissimilar from those used to make the Gregorian calendar that we use today.

POK-TA-POK

Along with various other Mesoamerican cultures, the Maya played a ball game (pok-ta-pok) based on the stars.

The court, which was bigger than a modern football field, is thought to have represented heaven, or the sky, and the ball symbolised the Sun. The aim of the game was for players to get the ball through hoops placed 6-9m (20-30ft) above the ground, using their bodies but not their hands or feet. The ball was made from rubber, suggesting that vulcanization (using other materials to make rubber more durable) occurred in Central America before Charles Goodyear supposedly invented the process in 1839.

DID YOU KNOW?

There was also a darker side to this sporting ritual as many historians believe the members of the losing team were sacrificed and their heads cut off!

THE INCA

At its peak, the Inca Empire was the largest of the South American kingdoms, stretching thousands of miles along the mountainous west coast of the continent. Despite the rugged and precipitous terrain, the empire thrived due to its many farming communities producing an abundance of food.

WHERE IN THE WORLD?

FARMING

They say that an army marches on its stomach and the long-term success of the Inca Empire was heavily reliant on its food production. The majority of workers in this society would have been farmers.

Despite a great deal of Inca territory being mountainous, farmers cut deep notches and canals into the cliffside to produce areas suitable for growing crops. The Inca also experimented with growing different varieties of fruit and vegetables, choosing the most hardy to plant each season. Many of the ancient varieties of potatoes, corn and quinoa are still grown by Peruvians today.

When Europeans invaded in the 16th century the Inca were rumoured to have had enough food within stores to last for 90 years.

MACHU PICCHU

The iconic ruins at the base of the Peruvian mountain known as Machu Picchu (Old Peak) were built during the 15th century. Archaeologists believe this collection of buildings functioned as a royal retreat where rulers and aristocrats could get away from the hustle and bustle of Inca life and enjoy some peace and quiet!

THE AZTECS

The Aztecs ruled much of Mexico in the 15th and 16th centuries, building grand structures and monumental temples from which to worship their many gods. Their largest city, Tenochtitlán was home to as many as 400,000 people at its busiest, but this civilisation began with just a few tribes settling on islands and shores of Lake Texcoco.

BIG CITY LIFE

Mexico City now sprawls across the landscape on the site where Tenochtitlán once stood. This ancient settlement grew to be successful because of its proximity to fresh water, allowing crops to be grown using irrigation channels, fish to be caught and drinking water to be readily available. Life could be sustained here for hundreds of thousands of people.

DID YOU KNOW?

War was commonplace in Aztec culture and a military profession was held in high regard. The jaguars and eagles were the highest-ranking military commanders and each had its own special uniform.

The Aztecs battled with unique clubs strewn with obsidian glass, fashioned into sharp edges even finer than the steel used to make swords! Some of the Aztec blades that archaeologists have discovered are still sharp to this day.

AZTEC CALENDAR

The Aztecs were devoutly religious and held many festivals in honour of their gods. In order to keep tabs on all of these occasions, they needed to keep track of time.

Many Aztec calendars were carved from stone, depicting the sun god – the most important god – at the very centre.

WHERE IN THE WORLD?

Tenochtitlán was home to hundreds of temples and decadent buildings including Montezuma II's palace, which was rumoured to have had in excess of 300 rooms.

DID YOU KNOW?
The number of Aztec people rose rapidly as Aztec tribes invaded neighbouring areas, imprisoning anyone they could find.

Sick and elderly prisoners were cast out and left to fend for themselves, others were executed in the form of religious offerings or enslaved, and some were adopted into regular society.

THE FALL OF A GREAT EMPIRE

The Aztec Empire collapsed shortly after Hernán Cortés, a Spanish conquistador (explorer), landed on South American shores in the early 16th century. His invasion began in 1519 when several hundred Spanish sailors explored and infiltrated the Yucatán Peninsula in Mexico, moving inland towards the great city of Tenochtitlán – the epicentre of the civilisation.

As Spanish forces stormed the city, the Aztec ruler Montezuma II was taken prisoner and eventually died in captivity. Much of the city was destroyed by the Spanish forces and many of the natives wiped out by the scourge of European diseases that had now been introduced.

TIMELINE

The dates in this timeline refer to when each civilisation was approximately founded.

NATIVE AMERICANS 11,000 BCE

AUSTRALIAN ABORIGINALS 50,000 BCE

NUBIANS 5000 BCE

MELANESIANS 40,000 BCE

OLMECS 1600 BCE

ANCIENT CHINESE 1600 BCE

BABYLONIANS 1792 BCE

MICRONESIANS 1100 BCE

POLYNESIANS 1500 BCE

AZTECS 1325 CE

MONGOLS 1206 CE

INCA 1100 CE

INDUS VALLEY
3300 BCE

SUMERIANS
3100 BCE

EGYPTIANS
3100 BCE

MINOANS
3000 BCE

ASSYRIANS
2000 BCE

AKKADIANS
2340 BCE

PHOENICIANS
3000 BCE

ANCIENT GREEKS
800 BCE

ROMANS
753 BCE

CELTS
700 BCE

Many of the ancient cultures and peoples on this timeline are extant today, including the Aboriginal Australians and Native Americans.

VIKINGS
793 CE

MAYA
300 CE

PERSIANS
539 BCE

WHAT CAME NEXT?

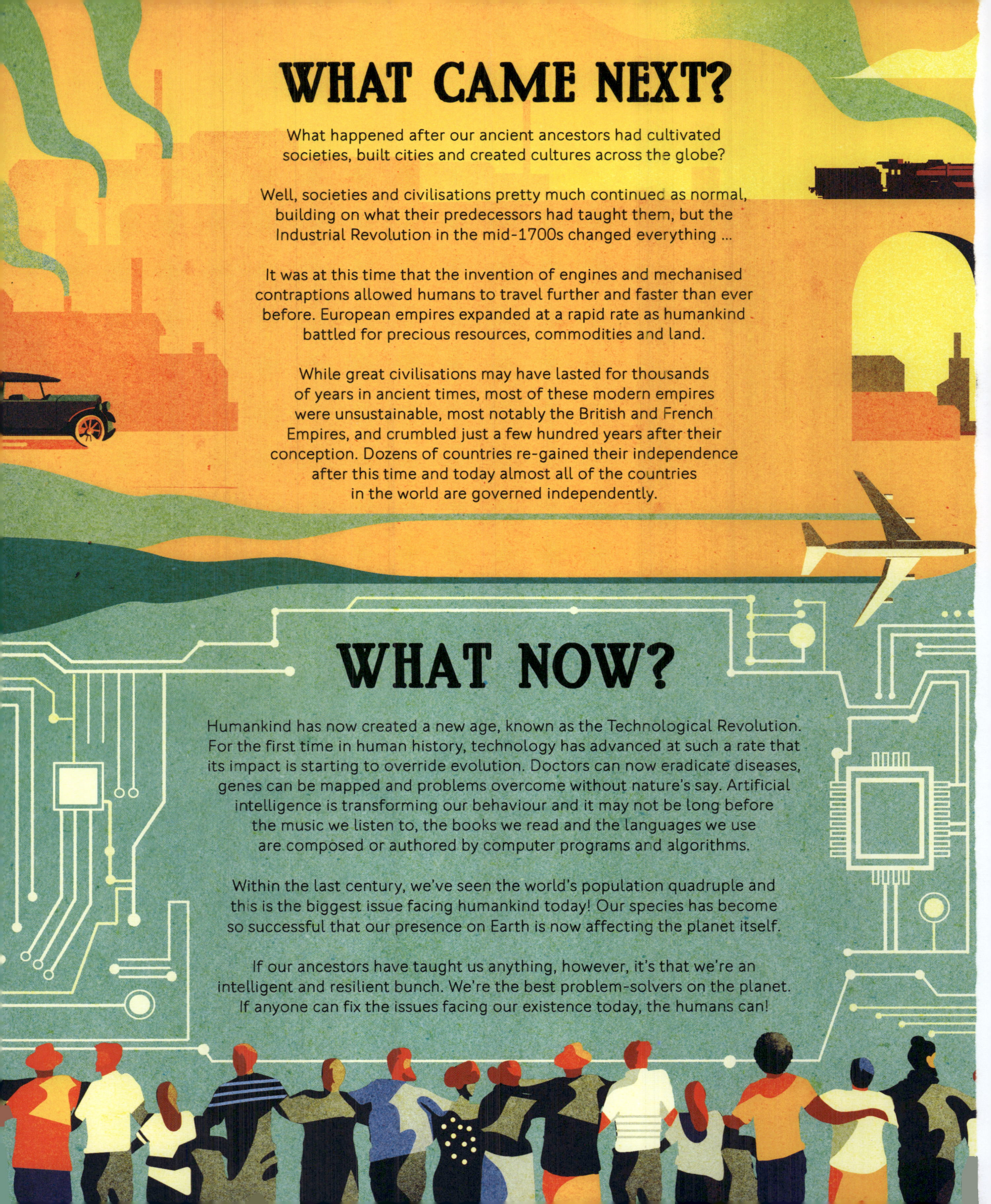

What happened after our ancient ancestors had cultivated societies, built cities and created cultures across the globe?

Well, societies and civilisations pretty much continued as normal, building on what their predecessors had taught them, but the Industrial Revolution in the mid-1700s changed everything …

It was at this time that the invention of engines and mechanised contraptions allowed humans to travel further and faster than ever before. European empires expanded at a rapid rate as humankind battled for precious resources, commodities and land.

While great civilisations may have lasted for thousands of years in ancient times, most of these modern empires were unsustainable, most notably the British and French Empires, and crumbled just a few hundred years after their conception. Dozens of countries re-gained their independence after this time and today almost all of the countries in the world are governed independently.

WHAT NOW?

Humankind has now created a new age, known as the Technological Revolution. For the first time in human history, technology has advanced at such a rate that its impact is starting to override evolution. Doctors can now eradicate diseases, genes can be mapped and problems overcome without nature's say. Artificial intelligence is transforming our behaviour and it may not be long before the music we listen to, the books we read and the languages we use are composed or authored by computer programs and algorithms.

Within the last century, we've seen the world's population quadruple and this is the biggest issue facing humankind today! Our species has become so successful that our presence on Earth is now affecting the planet itself.

If our ancestors have taught us anything, however, it's that we're an intelligent and resilient bunch. We're the best problem-solvers on the planet. If anyone can fix the issues facing our existence today, the humans can!

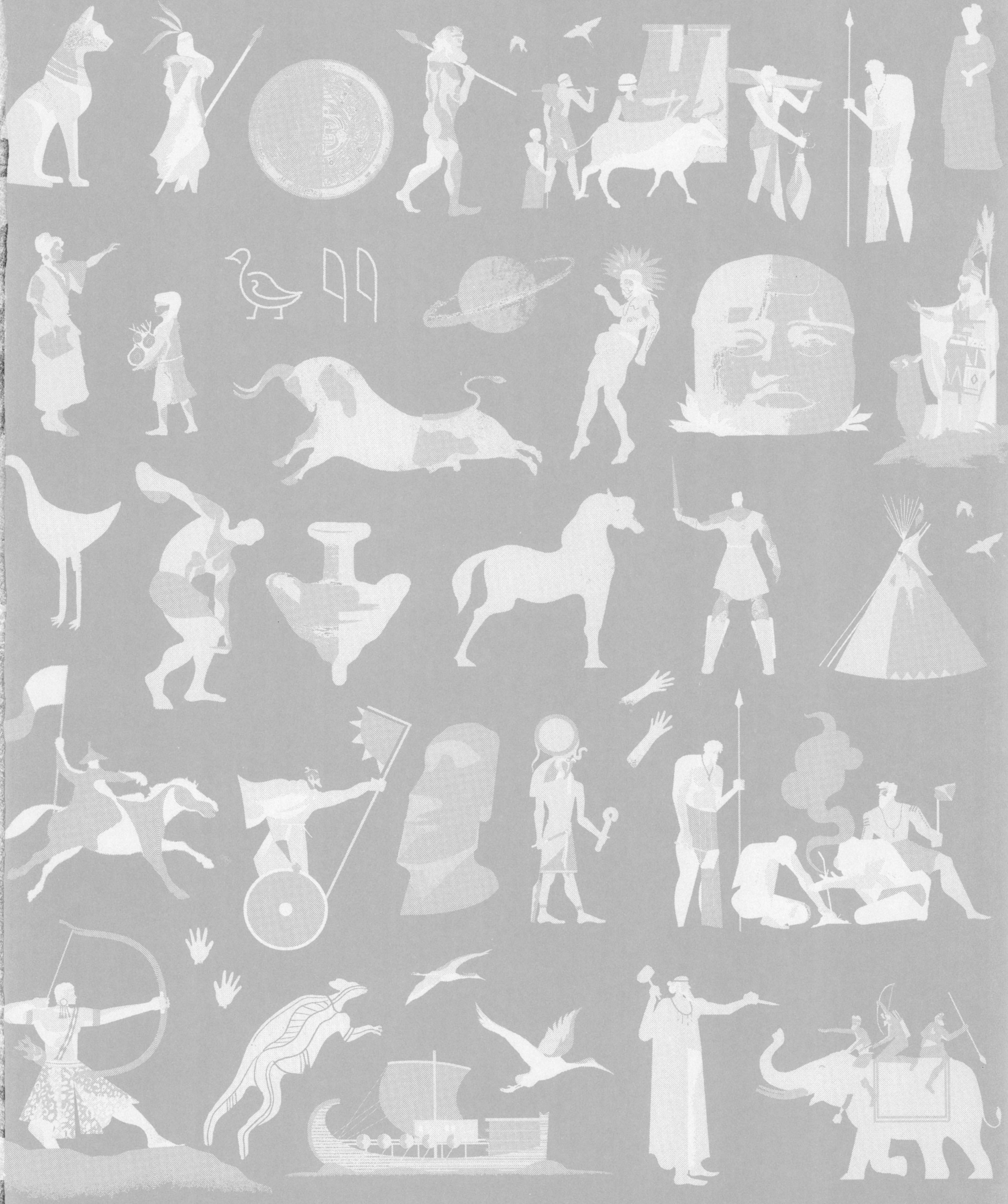